Out of the Valley

A Mestizo of Genres

D1519251

Out of the Valley
A Mestizo of Genres

Edited by:
Joyce Armstrong Carroll

With a Foreword by:
Pam Muñoz Ryan

ABSEY & CO.
SPRING, TX

Copyright © 2006

Library of Congress Cataloging-in-Publication Data

2 0 0 6 9 2 2 7 1 3

Out of the Valley
Out of the Valley /Out of the Valley —1st ed
p. cm.

ISBN 1-888842-49-0

Printed in the United States of America

Requests for permission to make copies
of any part of the work should be mailed to:

Permissions
Absey & Co. Inc.
23011 Northcrest
Spring, Texas 77389

Layout and Cover designed by Gracy Michelle Garcia Leal

Visit us at www.Absey.biz

Contents

Acknowledgments

First, I thank all of the New Jersey Writing Project in Texas trainers, trainees, teachers, and administrators from the school districts in the Rio Grande Valley: Edinburg, McAllen, Mercedes, Rio Grande City, La Joya, Donna, Edcouch-Elsa, and the NJWPT Demonstration Site District, Weslaco. Without the support from these districts and the good people who love and serve the students in these districts, this collection would never have borne fruit.

I am also indebted to Pam Muñoz Ryan for so graciously agreeing to write a Foreword for this collection. Indeed, with her own busy schedule of writing and speaking, she did not need to take on this additional task. Thus, her words are more than appreciated and stand as a tribute to her dedication to writing and to her culture.

To five special bilingual teachers in Alvin ISD, I am especially grateful. Their feedback on the hundreds of manuscripts was invaluable. I would be remiss not to thank each individually:

Plácida R. López
Tami Pérez
Rebecca Angulo Whitton
Flora Niznik
Maritza González

Fernando Castillo deserves applause for his help as does Elena Betancourt.

I want to thank Dee Ann Schovajsa for her meticulous typing of the manuscripts and Gracy Leal for the terrific layout and cover design. No book is complete without the help of an excellent editor—this book had Jill Elizabeth Aufill.

Elvira Ledesma Aguayo, however, receives top recognition for her painstaking reading and rereading of the manuscripts, checking the correctness of all the diacritic marks that are part of the Spanish language, and for compiling the glossary. Without EA (as she is lovingly addressed) this collection would lack the finesse it so deserves.

Foreword

Beginnings and Belongings

My life began in a valley in California, far away from the Rio Grande Valley in Texas, yet these selections triggered my own memories. How could that be? I did not know the world of these authors and they did not have knowledge of mine. What then, did we have in common?

We are Mexican and American, sharing a culture torn between two countries. We struggle with keeping, and letting go. We have deep roots and great affection for our beginnings and belongings and yet we have often moved on, or moved away. We value and respect our culture but are sometimes burdened by its changing dynamics.

The push and pull of a people finding their way is prevalent in this book. Here are legacies of hardships, challenges, and admitted idiosyncrasies. Here are tales of mutual aspirations and dreams–come–true. Not only do they reflect one people's journey, they also reflect our shared humanity.

Memories can be spent in many ways. They can be guarded with vigilance. They can be shared through oral retelling. They can be written down. Following are the chronicles of brave authors who chose to write them down, who mined their feelings and emotions so the next generation will remember the rich well of language and culture from which they came. Pay close attention. It's as if each writer is whispering, "Don't forget. Don't forget the sounds, tastes, sights, smells, and feel of our heritage."

Don't be surprised if one of these selections reminds you of your own beginnings and belongings. And when you find yourself rolling them around in your mind, as if you were savoring a long-lasting butterscotch candy on your tongue, consider the story that you might like to tell.

–Pam Muñoz Ryan

Out of the Valley:
A Mestizo of Genres
PREFACE

"The whole valley breathes and lives."
    --Pam Muñoz Ryan, *Esperanza Rising*

    This is a "world that we can call our own," this family space through which generations move, each bringing its gifts, handing down languages and stories, recipes for living, gathering around the kitchen table to serve one another...."
    --Pat Mora, *House of Houses*

    To edit this collection has been a dream of mine since I first came to the Rio Grande Valley over twenty years ago. I knew as did author Earl Shorris when he wrote in *The Life and Times of Mexico*, "There is a difference in the vicinity of the heart between Mexico and the United States." I felt it immediately. Palpable, this difference beats in the language and laughter of the people, it mixes in the flavor and colors of the food, it blends in the jumble of the cultures—in short, it pulsates with a uniqueness that is the Rio Grande Valley. To paraphrase Pam Muñoz Ryan, this difference gives the Valley its breath and life.
    In this living entity, called by Tom Miller, editor of *Writing on the Edge*, "the thin Third Country," I have found writers who cap-

ture this palatability, this singularity through poems, stories, memoirs, anecdotes, tributes, characterizations—all resonating with the laughter, joys, tragedies, passion, sorrows, and the pure everyday life of the border. Like the threads woven into the *rebozo*, the perfect symbol of *mestizo*, these threads form a perspective of the real people, the real lives in the Rio Grande Valley. I have long longed to be privileged to bind these threads into a whole.

This collection fulfills that dream, that longing, due to the openness and willingness of these writers to share.

Then in the editing I found even more richness—a fertile loam of language that rises as a commixture of Spanish and Spanish slang, English and English slang, intermingled proverbs and transposed prepositions that lifts the reader into levels of meaning that transcend the mere word. Some linguists call this "interference," an unflattering term, a negative; others label it "code-switching," suggesting that the writer cannot quite express the meaning fully in one language. Folly that! This intermingling of language enriches; it is an asset.

Actually, in literary history the use of the *bon mot* (F) was considered the sign of wit; peppering a piece of writing with words such as *Adytum* (Gr), or phrases such as *in situ* (Lat), or *in petto* (Ital) was expected as a sign of breadth of education. Throughout the offerings in this book, writers draw on their bilingualism, build upon it, reminding me of a quote I heard years ago, "A person is worth as many people as languages he or she speaks!" In Spanish, the *dicho* goes like this, *"Quien sabe dos lenguas, vale por dos."* "If you are bilingual, you count twice."

My hope is that this book will be welcomed by young readers to be used not only to extend the Valley outward to other cultures but also to enable Hispanic students geographically separated from their roots to re-embrace what is distinctively theirs. Further, I hope this collection will be read by adults who will find threads of their experiences woven into the fabric of the book. As Sandra Cisneros says, "Writing is like sewing together what I call these 'buttons,' these bits and pieces." Together, the writers in *Out of the Valley: A Mestizo of Genres* have sewn together buttons from the bits and pieces of their lives to share with you, the reader. Remember: *"Gozo comunicado crece."* "Shared joy grows."

—Joyce Armstrong Carroll, Ed.D., H.L.D.

" 'Shhh," he said. "You can only feel the earth's heartbeat when you are still and quiet.' ...She stared at Papa, not wanting to say a word. Not wanting to lose the sound. Not wanting to forget the feel of the heart of the valley."

—Pam Muñoz Ryan, *Esperanza Rising*

Mourning/Morning

Elvira Ledesma Aguayo

Several factors have converged to make my life more interesting: I took a nasty fall, injuring my left leg; Jesse, my husband, threw his back out on the following Monday morning; that same day I started a three-week writing class. And finally, the one factor that is a terrible constant: our beloved *Mamá* Beatriz at ninety is flirting with Alzheimer's.

This morning has been particularly hard. First, I wake up at 4:14 with an urgent need to go to the bathroom. I groan as I swing my left leg—the injured one—off the bed. I stick my feet into my 1 3/4-inch sandals—heaven forbid I walk barefoot or flatfooted on this blasted leg—and shuffle to the bathroom. I flip on the light and look at the leg. It resembles an unappetizing overstuffed sausage from knee to toes. Right now, it's all about the leg. I don't have hands or neck or eyes or even a *right* leg. It's all left leg with its varied dull and sharp pains taking turns coming to the forefront of consciousness. All along, I'm carrying on an internal conversation. *Yes, you can. Look, it's getting better. Okay now—not too much pressure on it. There, there, it's okay. Ooh! Look at all those colors... I wonder what would happen to that bruise if I stuck a straight pin in it? I guess I'd better not try that. Hmmm. Okay. Now, how do I lower myself here without—Okay, Okay, got it!"*

By this time, the urgency that woke me up has taken a hike to never-never land or la-la land or someplace, and I have to wait.

Then I hear it: the first call of the morning. It starts out faint, as if far away. "*¿Ya me levanto? ¿Me levanto ya?*" I hold my breath, almost afraid she can hear me. It's *Mamá* Beatriz, and her day has unofficially begun. From now until 7:00 A.M. she'll be asking every three to seven minutes if it's time to get up. And each time she asks is the first time, no matter how many replies she's had.

I don't answer. Instead, I hobble back to bed, having taken care of the bodily necessity that woke me up in the first place. I throw the pillows that had been holding the leg "above the heart" all night long off the bed with satisfaction. Darn thing didn't work anyhow; my leg has become more swollen overnight.

I go back to sleep, and wake again at 5:30. This time her voice is stronger, "*¿No hay gente? ¿Me levanto ya?*"

I go to the bedroom door, open it, and call down the stairs. "*Todavía no, Mamá. It's too early.*"

"*¿Es temprano? Así pensaba yo. Bueno. Ya me voy a acostar. Gracias. Me hablas, ¿eh?*"

"*Sí, Mamá, yo le hablo,*" I tell her. I can hear her muttering as she returns to her room.

I take my shower—not quickly, not possible with this leg—and get dressed. By this time, *Mamá* has called up three times again and is upset. I go to her room and tell her, "*Ya es hora, Mamita. Levántese y dése un baño.*"

"*Ya me bañé,*" she retorts. She's fully dressed in clothes Jesse set out for her last night.

"*No, Mamita, no se ha bañado.*"

"*Y tú, ¿cómo sabes?*" she challenges.

"*Porque se oye cuando corre el agua, Mamá. Ándele, báñese antes que se levante Chuy.*" I walk out of her room and go to the kitchen.

Three minutes later she comes out. "*Bueno, ya me voy a bañar.*"

I try to keep my voice light. "*Bueno, Mamita.*"

So I go on about my business, putting on my face, combing my hair—all the while hoping my leg doesn't start screaming at me with tiny titillations of torture. (Okay, okay, so I exaggerate.)

Oh--did I mention my husband threw his back out of whack on Monday? You can imagine. We're living in a house of moans and *ya-me-levantos*.

Mamá finally takes her bath. Then, while I'm packing some product to send to a customer, she drops a picture and the glass breaks. My husband, while trying to clean up after her, messes up his back again. He comes out and calls to her because it's time to take me to my class.

Mamá comes out. There's chalky white stuff all over her face. She's taken the Secret® deodorant stick I bought her just yesterday and broken off pieces to rub on over her face and arms.

Jesse cracks. *"Mamá, ¿qué hizo?"* She stares at him blankly, not understanding why she's being scolded.

I take her by the hand. *"Venga conmigo, Mamá,"* as I lead her to her bathroom. I find the half-used deodorant on the vanity and put it away, up high where she can't reach it.

I moisten a face towel and wipe the white off her face as I ask her why she did it.

She says, *"Pos no sé.* It's just that this mind is no good any more, and all I do is dumb and stupid things. *No sirvo pa'nada."*

"Ya está lista, Mamá. Vámonos." It's already 7:44, and I have to get to school.

"¿Te vas a ir? ¿Por qué?" She demands. "Why don't you stay?"

"Nomás voy al trabajo. Ándele, vamos." We have her sit in the front passenger seat.

The visor is down so I can see her face in the mirror. She does-n't know I'm watching. She's trying to replay the morning in her mind because Jesse mentions that she has deodorant on her arms too.

"It won't hurt her," I reassure him.

Her mouth turns down and her lips quiver. I don't want her to hurt. I lean forward and massage her head.

"A lo mejor hallas piojos," she jokes.

"No creo; I won't find any lice on you!" I respond.

The bad moment is broken.

Mamita

Elvira Ledesma Aguayo

As she lay dying,
we tended to her body,
my sister, our cousin, and I.
We did what she could not
but would have:
washed her hair and combed it,
bathed her top to bottom
and rubbed scented lotion on
her arms, her legs, her bosom—
She did not say a word
nor spare us a look—
she could not—
but her brow relaxed
and a whisper of a smile
played on her lips.
As she lay dying,
we tended to her spirit
her *familia* (related by blood
and not)—with prayers
and *cantos* and *cuentos* and jokes—
She loved jokes!
We blessed her over
and over as she had blessed us
with her love.

We touched her with fingertips
and lips bearing our very souls.
A touch of the divine
loving and beloved
poised in the moment
poised at eternity.
As she lay living,
there but no longer there,
We tended our spirits:
orphaned we cried and
laughed and sang and cried.
Our hearts were numb;
she was set free.
We rejoiced as we mourned
walking in shadows.
She touched us with light.
We hurt, we praised,
we said *adios*
and *hasta luego*.
She has become
un vaso nuevo.

Lessons
Marta Isela Aguayo

The hallway beckoned; a force unseen propelled my clumsy feet to move against the squeaky clean, disturbingly white floor. Ahead, a window—an escape—loomed, teasing me, offering a glimpse at what lay beyond the suffocating walls, though knowing I could never really take it up on its offer. I walked mechanically, fearfully, clutching my well worn leather backpack, refusing to hazard a glance at my sister, lest I fall and never get up again. This was the moment of weakness and strength, a moment I would have given anything to avoid.

"This is it," my sister whispered solemnly, gesturing at the only open door in the wing. I drew a long breath and squeezed my eyes shut, scanning my memory banks for happier times and forcing them forward until they tickled my eyelids. Such whimsical little memories. Nearing the room, I could smell a blend of familiar fragrances—Old Spice met Happy and cross-pollinated with Polo—worn on skin both young and old. And more—an antiseptic, uncaring smell clung to the air with a vice grip, unwilling to yield to more pleasant smells. It was in charge and soon it would give way to something far more severe.

I stood at the threshold and stared. There she was, her hand encased lovingly in another's gentle hands. But I could see nothing but her. There she was, being spoken to in hushed tones. But I could hear nothing but her. My eyes sought hers, desperately yearning to make a connection, hoping she could finally see me. It had been so long since she knew me.

My backpack fell down, hanging haphazardly off my forearm. I felt it drop to the floor and heard the smack of the buckles against the tile. Leaning over, I pressed my lips against her forehead, feeling the heat practically sear through the skin. *"Welita,"* I whispered into her ear, *"Soy Marta. Aquí estoy."* A flash of recognition flickered through her eyes, though nothing came out of her mouth–the oxygen mask made sure of that. But she knew me. For the last time, she knew me.

Choking back the tears, I straightened to stand, finally taking stock of the room, suddenly remembering my manners. Round robin I went, following my sister's lead, enveloping others in embraces, trying to stave off the utter despair we all felt with the cold comfort of warm hugs and kisses. We are family, after all— it's what we do. I tried not to succumb to the anguish as I worked my way back to her side, claiming a squeaky chair as my perch by the chirping heart machine. Oh, how I wanted to stay there forever, just watching and hoping. Because even then, even when I knew it was the end, I still hoped it would get better. Silly human.

For hours I sat and stood and sat again, watching waves of people come through the door all wearing expressions of solemnity, all knowing the gravity of what would soon take place. I resented their resignation and secretly longed for it.

As day swept into evening, I felt my heart harden to the truth. And I began to count. The death watch had begun.

More goodbyes spoken in whispers and cries in that small cell of a room, some filled with joy and gratitude, others rife with guilt and remorse. There are all kinds of goodbyes, it seems, and sometimes it has less to do with the person that's leaving than with the person who's staying. Yet another lesson she taught me, even as she moved listlessly on the bed, covered by a sterile white sheet, struggling for breath.

There wasn't enough space in that whole hospital to fit us all—the angry, the complacent, the loving, the fearful, the strong, the weak. Too much conflict, not enough beds. So we spread out as best we could. I found solace in the waiting area down the hall from the dying room. Newspapers sat carelessly on the edge of vinyl seats, while family members milled around in groups, eager to make idle chitchat in lieu of speaking truths. I knew the truth already, so why rehash it? I sat uncomfortably, my legs spread wider than decency permitted, my arms crossed against my torso, and I stared at the clock that hung in between the two elevator doors. Tick. Tock. Tick. Tock. Everything about the place taunted and teased. Every time the elevator opened its doors in lethargy, unfamiliar familiar faces would emerge with glazed eyes and mascara-tracks running down puffy cheeks. Every time I would lead them, hearing the unpleasant squeaks of rubber soles and the click clack of sensible pumps against the now reviled tile, and every time I would leave them, to relieve their grief, to make promises, to ask for forgiveness, or to make peace.

There were false alarms, premature outpourings of uncontrollable grief when the steady beep of the infernal heart machine dissipated suddenly. But just as quickly, it would return, filling the breathless room with unexpressed relief and frustration. My father, most beloved son of my *Welita*, leaned over the bed, bringing his tender mouth to her ear and whispering words of comfort, words of devotion, words of God. I knew these words so well. They were said by him only when his absolute faith transcended every selfish, human instinct. He knew it was time. He wanted her to be free. And in those moments watching my father, so loving with his mother, I wanted her to be free not just for her, but for him as well.

Death had its own timetable. So we waited some more. I sat and wondered whether I would become emotional, whether I would need help. I walked out of the room, overhearing my *Tío* swear to himself and others that he would be strong for my *Tía*; he had to be strong for everyone else. I vowed silently, to myself and to my *Welita*, that I, too, would be strong. Another lesson learned.

The heart machine began to wane. Someone–a cousin, an aunt–called us to enter. There we all stood, in a misshapen semi-circle, her bed flanked by all her children, half of her grandchildren, and some of her great grandchildren. We all waited, watching carefully, trying to memorize the moment. Then it was over. Her last breath drawn without fanfare, her eyes closed gently, her hands at her sides. No longer listless, no longer in pain, no longer present in that tiny room that held no secrets to the past or promise of the future. *Welita* was dead. My heart constricted and refused to release, even as I moved into action, breaking people's falls, wiping away tears. The cries of anguish filled the room, and I was powerless to stop them, though grateful that they could do what I would not allow myself to do.

"Get some water," someone called out. "Pull up a chair. Set her here. Make her comfortable. Where are the tissues?" In the end, just words to keep the animalistic shrieks from taking complete control over everyone.

As the incredulous cries turned to silent acceptance, I navigated my way back into the room, to my *Welita's* side. Kneeling, I stroked her cold hand tenderly, knowing that I would never again feel her squeeze my hand in return. I looked up and saw my *Tía* gingerly removing tape from my *Welita's* arm. She felt my gaze, saying softly, "We have to do this gently. If the nurses do it, they'll rip the skin off. I won't let them rip the skin off." I nodded, understanding the importance of this ritual. I looked down at the hand I was stroking and began to remove the IV and tape that stood in sharp contrast to her smooth skin. Slowly, I peeled the transparent tape, seeing her thin skin rise from the force. I bit my lip and held my breath, praying that I could finish it. Extracting the IV needle from her vein, I marveled at the trickle of blood left in its wake. How odd it was that she was dead but still able to bleed. I patted the skin, smoothing it, tracing the patterns of her veins. I bent my head and kissed the hand that had held me, spanked me, loved me, known me. It was the end of her journey and this was my last act of love.

Walking away from that hallway that had earlier held so much power over me, I could almost hear her low voice whispering soft-ly against the recycled air, teaching me, yet again, another les-son—the most important lesson—love doesn't end with death; love begins when life no longer stands in the way. Slipping my arms into the straps of my backpack, I left with my sister at my side, knowing the truth but desperately rebelling against it.

"*Del Dicho al Hecho...*"
Brenda Avila

"**A** *fuerzas ni los zapatos entran*," declared my mother, after I had explained my dilemma.

With a puzzled look, I asked her, "What do shoes have to do with my love life?" *Mamá* laughed and went on to explain what her words of wisdom literally meant—that was my first encounter with a *dicho.*

Dichos, or Spanish adages, have been around for many generations, and if you happen to be a Mexican-American woman as I am, you can thank your *mamá* for introducing you to them. As a matter of fact, if you are Mexican-American, your *mamá* probably first heard of *dichos* from her *mamá*, and she from hers, and so on. Whatever the case, *dichos* are a type of expression that sneak up on you, and if you aren't prepared and caught by surprise, they make you want to scream out to your mother, "Cut to the chase, Mom!"

According to Bernardo R. Nieto, "*Dichos* are an intricate part of Mexican culture" (*El Paso Times*, "Borderlands," Spring, 1995, Vol. 11:14). *Dichos* are proverbs, or sayings in Spanish, which express insights, observations, or judgments based on life experiences. *Dichos*, or general truths, are found in many different cultures, including Mexican, Chinese, Portuguese, Greek, and American. In the United States *dichos* are sometimes confused with idioms.

Linguarama (www.linguarama.com) defines "an idiom as a group of words which, when used together, have a different meaning from one which the individual words have." For example, according to the idiom site (www.idiomsite.com), "cut to the chase," actually means "get to the point," a movie term from the 1920s. Regardless of a person's age, idioms tend to produce the same reaction when heard for the first time. In my experience, as an educator of young children, students' reactions to idioms almost always commence with amusement followed by perplexity; whereas, *dichos* are little aphorisms conveying succinctly little lessons that are easy to understand.

Recently I had the opportunity to celebrate a birthday in the company of the two wisest Mexican-American women I know—my mother and grandmother—and became amused at their conversation. As *Mamá* and *Guelita* sat outdoors discussing family matters and catching up, I noticed those cultural "gems of truth" being tossed around simultaneously and automatically. Witnessing this encounter proves Nieto's statement, "*Dichos* are passed down from one generation to another by word of mouth."

"*Recuerda que no eres monedita de oro para caerles bien a todos,*" *Guelita* Concha advised my mother during their conversation, but before my mother could begin to respond, *Guelita* added, "*El que a buen arbol se arrima, buena sombra lo cobija.*" *Mamá's* smile said it all. According to Marc Simmons in his article, "Trail Dust: Wise and Earthy Spanish Proverbs Make Clear, '*Vale más saber que tener*,'" *dichos* "have a way of expressing a great deal with an economy of words" (*The Santa Fe New Mexican*, May 7, 2005). Yet for *Mamá*, an educated retired accountant, those few words spoken by *Guelita* Concha conveyed a common sense lesson that she not only understood but treasured.

Dichos, types of verbal treasures, enhance our lives, enrich our relationships, reflect our culture, strengthen our roots, and often mirror the values of our society. Octavio Ballesteros' *Mexican Sayings: The Treasure of a People* is an anthology, representing a spectacular collection of *dichos*, a treasure of knowledge.

Ballesteros explains that *dichos* remind us where we come from, offer promise and hope, and are wiser than any of us.

"Del plato a la boca, se cae la sopa," the first *dicho* my mother ever heard, loosely translates "no matter how close to sealing a deal a person may be, nothing is certain in this life, and everything can fall apart in a split second." Although simple, these words of wisdom transformed her life as well as my own. However, more valuable than gold is what those nuggets of truth represent in our everyday lives: shaping, modifying, consoling, and perhaps even saving us from mistakes.

When I was a teenager, to prevent me from hanging around with the wrong crowd, *Mamá* warned, *"El que con lobos se junta, a aullar se enseña."* If new acquaintances seemed too friendly, *"Caras vemos, corazones no sabemos"* meaning we can see their outsides, but we can't see their insides. Because I may have thought too highly of myself at one point, *"Lo que menos puedes ver, en tu casa lo has de tener"* became *Mamá's* saying to bring me back to reality. Matters of the heart? *Mamá* had plenty to say about that, *"Cuando el río suena, es que piedras lleva,"* a cautionary *dicho* for when I heard a rumor pertaining to my significant other; however, if my significant other did me wrong, *Mamá's* words became, *"Ojos que no ven, corazon que no siente,"* or, *"El que ríe al último, ríe mejor."* "What you don't know can't hurt you," and "He who laughs last, laughs the hardest," words that made a world of difference for me.

As I sit and reflect on the research I conducted to put this piece together—the library, the bookstore, the computer—I came to realize that although full of knowledge, none could offer me what two Mexican-American women gave me during that birthday party—a constant reminder of where I come from. As I try to find my place in this melting pot of cultures, I see that no matter where my life may take me, *dichos* will forever give me a permanent belonging place.

Barefoot Dreams

JoLynn Balli

My mom's story is the same as everyone else's here in the Valley. By the time she was six, she was picking cotton in the West Texas fields. Work started at 5:30 in the morning and continued until sunset. She rarely had a chance to enjoy the things most kids enjoy. She never played kickball, or soccer, or hopscotch. She never played dress-up, or teacher, or even learned how to ride a bike. She never learned to swim or float in the water.

What she did learn to do was weed her way through a cotton field infested with bees and snakes. She learned to walk with her back bent over all day while she carried a heavy brown potato bag overflowing with cotton. Mom learned about racism and abuse before she learned her ABC's and 123's.

There are hundreds of stories she can tell at any given moment about her childhood as a poor uneducated Mexican. But the one I remember, the one that angers me to this day, is the one about the shoes.

"Everyone was poor at that time," Mom states without any kind of resentment in her voice, "especially my family. We were happy that way. I never knew any other way."

As the seventeenth child in her family, she often went without many of the things her parents considered luxuries, including shoes. When she was eight she was taken along with her classmates to the white building on 17th Street to sing for members of the city council. There she stood, long black Indian hair, parted down the middle. She wore a white oversized hand-me-down *vestido* stained with wear from whomever it belonged to last. It was her best dress, her only dress.

Placed in the back of the room, behind even the tallest of boys, she went unnoticed. Small, dark, and barefoot she sang with pride, *"Estas son las mañanitas que cantaba el rey David."* She belted out every word of the song in her dirty hand-me-down dress, feet white with dirt from the schoolyard. My poor mother, who never knew the difference, smiled as she sang. She gleamed with pride when the audience stood up in their polished expensive shoes and gave the class a standing ovation. When it was over, she was shuffled out of the building, into the rain and mud, and onto the school bus. Back at the schoolyard she was dismissed, and without anyone noticing, she walked home alone and barefoot in the rain.

She would not return for the next forty years.

This has been a good day, she thought. It was the first time anyone ever stood up and acknowledged anything she had ever done. Soon after that the family traveled to Oklahoma to continue working, and Mom became a drop-out at age eight.

As the years crept by, she struggled long and hard to return to school. While I was away at college, Mom began her own journey and started night school with the undying support of my father. Soon she even went to college, and when she graduated, I sat in my seat in the auditorium glowing with pride. When they called her name "Abeldia Olivo Balli," our entire family stood up, tears in our eyes, and cheered so loud we lost our voices. *She did it,* I thought. Mom finally did something for herself, and that has made all the difference in my own understanding of life. I have learned through Mom that any dream is attainable—that desire is all you need to make it come true. That is the greatest of all gifts.

Ana's Story

Sara Barrera

My sister-in-law, Ana, is the storyteller of our family. I have spent many hours in the living room of my *suegra's* house, with the rest of the family all around, listening to Ana tell her stories. One of our favorites (it has been told many times) is the story of the time she lost her underwear. This story never fails to leave us laughing.

Ana was just a young woman, newly married at the tender age of sixteen. She was pregnant with her first child, which is no surprise because Ana is always pregnant in her stories (she gave birth to seven children in a little over ten years). Anyway, she and her husband were both young and like most newlyweds a little short of money. She was so proud of herself because she had managed to save a little money by purchasing herself some maternity underwear at the *pulga* instead of spending much more for a better pair from WalMart.

One day while she was at the grocery store, she began to regret her penny-pinching ways. She was standing in the line at M. Rivas grocery in Donna when she felt the elastic of her underwear snap. Not sure what to do, she walked out of the store clutching huge bags of groceries in each arm. She gasped as she then felt the *calzones* start to slip down. She puffed out her stomach in a vain attempt to keep them up, or at least to slow their descent. She was wearing a dress, so she knew this could be disastrous. For a ways, she tried to waddle, holding her legs together from the knees up to keep her underwear up. She also clutched the grocery bags tighter to her side hoping they would hold up the loose underwear. She could just imaging how she looked. There were a few old men sitting on benches off to the side watching people pass by. She was painfully aware of their presence.

She battled with a decision. Should I drop my groceries to save the underwear, or do I drop the underwear to save the groceries? She thought about the embarrassment losing her underwear would cause. Her new young husband was watching her approach as he waited in the truck. What if he saw? Then she thought about how she had just spent $20 in groceries and swiftly made up her mind.

Stepping to the side between two vehicles, she wiggled her hips a little, and the underwear made a swift trip to the ground. Then she calmly stepped out of the *calzones*, kicking them neatly under the car to the right. She stepped back into the row and walked casually to the truck and climbed in next to her husband.

He asked her, "What were you doing over there?"

"Oh nothing," she replied nonchalantly. "I just thought I saw a dollar on the ground, but it was nothing."

He smiled at her and said, "I got a good one. Always trying to get money for us."

She smiled at her success in coming away from the situation squeaky clean. The sun was shining. She had a handsome husband by her side and a beautiful baby on the way. Life was good.

On the way home her husband asked her, "Do you need to go anywhere else?

"Yes," she replied. "Stop by the *pulga*. I need to buy some new *calzones*."

The Clueless Assassin

Sara Barrera

Noe Barrera couldn't understand what all the fuss was about. For weeks all people could talk about was that the President of the United States was coming to the Valley.

"So did you watch *las noticias* last night, *comadre?*"

"No, what did they say, *Panchita?*"

"That *el Presidente* Bill Clinton is going to pass right through 1015 on his way to some fancy dinner in McAllen."

"Really? I hope some crazy drunk doesn't hit him there on the corner of Mile 12. You know there was another accident there again two nights ago."

"Well, that can't happen. The newslady said that they are going to block off all the roads connecting to 1015, and nobody will be allowed to drive on it until he goes by. They also said that people weren't supposed to stand around on the sides of the road or anything."

"Well, how do they expect to keep folks from doing that? You've seen how they stand around and gawk whenever there's an accident. Imagine how it'll be when the president comes through?"

"I don't know, *comadre*. I hear there's going to be a lot of police out on the roads."

All this talk didn't really faze Noe. Nothing much interrupted his routine. You see, Noe was a twenty-year-old man with the mind of a seven-year-old. Everyone in the *colonia* knew this and accepted it. You could say he was one of its fixtures. You could always see him riding his bike up and down FM1015 between Miles 11 and 12. Sometimes he just hung outside Tiny's Convenience Store talking to anyone who came by, a real friendly sort, well-liked by all. His dad would often compare him to a hooker because he said that Noe would just wait around for someone to come pick him up to take him for a ride into town. He never did learn to read and write much, but he was real good with his hands. He could build a pretty decent birdcage, and he was an expert when it came to getting the knots out of fishing line. He lived with his mom, who took good care of him, so he didn't have to work, but he would sometimes do odd jobs for people just to keep himself busy and earn some spending money.

The day the whole Valley was waiting for finally arrived. As predicted, county police cruisers, black and white Texas State Trooper cars, and any other vehicle with lights on top of it were lined up and down 1015, waiting for President Clinton to come through. People anxiously peeked out windows. Small groups huddled in front lawns excitedly talking, waiting, and watching. Curious children were shooed into backyards by nervous mothers. A few of the braver citizens stood on the sides of the road ready to dash into yards whenever police cars passed by.

In the midst of all this commotion, Noe, oblivious to all that was going on, tried to decide what he felt like doing.

I guess I could just ride on over to Tiny's and see what's up. Maybe the soda man will come by again and give me another free coke. Oh wait, I know, I'll get the new pellet gun I bought at the pulga and go hunt some birds. Now where is it? I know I left it here behind the door.

"*Ma' dónde chingáos esta mi* pellet gun?"

"*No sé hijo.* Remember you can't go outside today. The President's coming."

"*N 'hombre. Puro pedo.*"

Oh, here it is in Mamá's closet. I wonder why she put it in here? I'll just walk down the street to Lalo's to see if he wants to come with me.

Meanwhile, the rest of the *colonia* was still waiting impatiently to catch a glimpse of the President's motorcade.

"Do you see anything yet, *Panchita?*"

"No, *comadre*. Just a bunch of police cars. Kids, get back away from that road or I'm going to call the police and tell them to arrest you! *¡Andale!*"

"*Ay*, look over there! What are all those police cars doing in front of the Barrera's?"

"I don't know. I'll get one of the kids to find out. Raulito, run over there and see if you can find out what's going on."

The scandal was all anyone could talk about for days.

"So, did you find out what happened at the Barrera's, *comadre?*"

"*Sí, comadre*. Raulito said that it was just Noe Barrera. He decided to go bird hunting. He was walking out with his pellet gun, can you believe that?"

"No! And then...?"

"Well, a state trooper was passing by and saw him with the gun and called for back-up. They thought he was going to assassinate the *Presidente.*"

"*Ay*, Noe! What was he thinking? *Pero* everyone knows that Noe is harmless."

"Well, apparently, *they* didn't know that because they were going to arrest him, but can you believe that when they asked him if he wanted to shoot Bill Clinton, he asked 'Bill who?' He didn't even know who they were talking about. Poor *Doña* Elvira! She came out and almost died when she saw all those cops around her *hijo.*"

"I can imagine. And now?"

"Well, I'm not sure because some cop ran Raulito off, but I don't think they arrested him."

"How do you know this *comadre?*"

"Well, I watched *las noticias* and they didn't say anything about it, so I'm just guessing."

"*Ay* Panchita! You and your *noticias!*"

Machismo

Sara Barrera

Sometimes the macho Mexican attitude is too much for me to bear. I had lived with my mother- and father-in-law for about four months when I finally had to speak my mind.

"*Suegra*, why do you do everything for him like that?"

"What do you mean, *hija*?"

"Well, you do everything around here while he just lays in his room all day, playing that old guitar or watching T.V. You cook for him; you clean his house; you iron his clothes, and I hear you get up at night when he wants you to run get him a glass of water. He's got two legs. Why don't you make him get it himself?"

"*Ay, hija*. That's just the way it's done. I guess I don't really like it, but you know what they say about old dogs. We're both just used to the old system. I'm sure it will be different with you and my son."

"That's for sure."

Later that day, I was sitting in my room reading when I heard my *suegro* yelling, "Elvirrra! Elvirrra!" He was getting louder and louder with each *grito*. I looked out the window and I could see my *suegra* outside mowing the lawn. I knew she couldn't hear him over the roar of the mower, but I also knew that my *suegro* could see her through his window. What the heck was the matter with him now? "Elvira, *ven!*"

Finally, having heard enough, I decided to get up to go see what he needed. Maybe there was something seriously wrong. He certainly sounded as if he was getting desperate. I rounded the corner, and poked my head into his room. He was reclining on the bed with the television blaring on some Spanish station, girls dancing half-naked on a stage.

"*¿Necesitas algo, Suegro?*"

"*Sí, mija. Apaga la luz, por favor.*

I calmly flipped the switch and walked out of the room, shaking my head. Oh well, at least he's not *my* husband.

Now, years later, I wish I had understood the concept "Like father, like son."

Money Doesn't Grow on Trees
Alfredo and Sara Barrera

My mother decided that it was time for us to learn the value of a dollar. We had become lazy children who didn't know what it was to work for a living. Ungrateful wretches, we spent our days watching television and running rampant around the neighborhood. She complained that we asked for money too often. She would tell us, *"¿Qué creen? ¿Que el dinero crece en árboles?"* What do you think? That money grows on trees?

I guess this made her stop and think because one day she informed us that she had found us a job picking oranges, and we all had to go. This included me (aged six), my sister Delia (eight), Ana (twelve), plus my brothers Noe (ten), David (fifteen), and Joe (seventeen). She made us all go to bed early the night before as we would have to get an early start.

I remember the excitement in the room where we all slept. *Mamá* had already told us what we would be doing and assured us that we would get paid for our work. It would be our first real job. We stayed up discussing all the oranges we were going to pick, and all the candy and *cohetes* we were going to buy with all the money we would earn. That the work would be hard never once crossed our minds.

I woke up while it was still dark outside to the smell of homemade *tortillas* and the sounds of *Mamá* yelling for us to hurry up.

We all hurried out of the house and piled into our old van. How could I ever forget that van? It was a faded red Dodge with only two tattered seats in the front. The rest of the van was bare. *Papá* had installed a homemade bench behind the driver's seat where we would all perch precariously as seatbelts were unheard of in our family. We would always rush to try to be the first in the van because the rear passenger-side window was missing and during the hot summer months being first in the van meant a nice fresh breeze. In the winter being first meant you got to avoid the window and laugh at the slower brother or sister who had to huddle in the frigid air. Usually the last one to make it to the van was my brother Noe who was just slow at everything.

We arrived at a large orange orchard outside Weslaco, not far from where we lived. Trucks and cars were parked up and down along the side of the road. Large trucks were unloading big wooden boxes that *Mamá* said we would fill with oranges. My mother herded us into a straight line and told us that we had to wait for *El Patrón*. He would assign us a row of trees to harvest.

After a few minutes, a short fat Mexican waddled up to us. "What family are you?"

"We're the Barrera family," my mother answered.

"Oh yes, you've been assigned the fourth row from that end. When you fill up the boxes, just come over here and ask for more." He hurried away without giving my mother a chance to ask any questions, which I think she wanted to do as she had a funny look on her face. She just shook her head and gave us a brave smile.

"I guess he's very busy. We need to get busy too. *¡Ándale güercos!* Let's go"

We all started picking the first tree. Once we had cleared the lower branches, we ran into our first problem.

"*Mamá*, how do we get the oranges from the top of the tree?" my brother David asked.

"I don't know, *hijo*." She considered his question for a minute then said, "Joe, go ask *El Patrón* for a ladder. Everyone else has one."

Joe came back with a ladder that started a whole new set of problems. My brothers all began to fight over who would get to climb the ladder. *Mamá* quickly stopped the fighting by giving the first tree to Joe. He climbed up and shook the tree. All the oranges came raining down. My sister Delia started howling because one orange hit her on top of the head. The rest of us laughed at her until *Mamá* gave us "the look."

"Get to work, *wewones!*" We quickly complied. This was easy! We just had to run around picking them up off the ground.

After what seemed like ten hours later, it didn't seem so easy. We were all exhausted, and we were all sick of hearing Noe whine because *Mamá* wouldn't let him climb the ladder. You see, Noe is kinda slow. He's okay at most things, but he's not very coordinated. He was mad that David and Joe were having all the fun. The girls and I never even considered asking to climb the tall ladder. We knew that would never happen.

We were also starving. In the van on the way to the orchard that morning we had eaten all of the food that Mama had packed for our lunch. When *Mamá* found out what we had done she was so mad she called us "*¡Cabrones!*" and said that a little hunger would do us good.

Then Joe came up with his "brilliant" plan. He told *Mamá* that the picking would go much faster if we split up. He somehow got us another ladder, and he suggested that he and David go down about five trees or so, and they would work their way back to us. I guess Mom was pretty tired by this time because she failed to catch the conniving glint in Joe's eyes. He was up to something and no way was I going to be left out.

"*Mamá*, I want to go with them," I whined. "They'll need someone to pick up the oranges off the ground." I ignored the murderous look David shot me.

"Okay, *mijo*. Go help your brothers," my mother agreed. Joe sent me a look that said, "You're going to pay for this," but I didn't care. I thought I was so smart.

When we got a few trees away, David and Joe began eating

oranges they had stuffed in their pockets. "I don't think we're supposed to eat the oranges." I looked around nervously, expecting to see *El Patrón* coming to get us.

"What? Is the little baby scared? Why don't you run back to Mommy?" David taunted.

After about ten minutes without lightning striking my brothers dead for their sin, my hunger got the best of me, and I asked for an orange too.

About five oranges later, we decided to start working. Joe and David climbed up a tree, but they just gave it a shake and then sat down, Joe on a branch, and David on the top rung of the ladder. "Come on Freddie. Pick 'em up," sneered Joe, as he pulled out a cigarette and began smoking. For the next hour, I ran around picking up oranges for my two lazy older brothers. I should have known better than to follow them.

Finally, when the sun was setting, we came to the end of the long row of orange trees. We were all so tired we just collapsed on the grass at the end of the row. I didn't think I would be able to move again. My sin of stealing oranges had come back to haunt me in the shape of an upset stomach. While we all laid there, *Mamá* went to get *El Patrón*. He walked back with her.

"We have finished picking all the trees, *señor*."

"¿*Qué*? What have you done? You weren't supposed to pick every tree. You were only supposed to pick every other one. I thought you said that you've done this before."

"No, no *señor*. I told you that I have worked the fields, but we always traveled out to California to work in the grapes. Since my husband's accident we haven't been able to travel."

"Thank God for that," I could hear Ana whisper to Delia.

Whatever *El Patrón* was going to say, we will never know because at that moment we heard Noe scream. While we weren't looking he had snuck off and climbed a ladder that was perched against the last tree in the row. He had gotten all the way to the top of the tree when he lost his balance and came crashing down. We all raced to his side. He was all cut up from the thorns of the orange tree and his right arm was bent into a funny angle. He was making a funny keening noise, like a *chicharra*. *Mamá* quickly grabbed him up, and we all ran to the van with *El Patrón* running along after us, yelling that perhaps we'd better not come back again tomorrow.

On the way to the hospital I sat up front next to *Mamá* while the others sat in the back with Noe. He was now whimpering like my dog Buster when his hind legs were run over by that *raspa* truck. Buster had made it, so I knew that Noe would too, but I was worried about *Mamá*. She drove along, not saying a word, but tears streamed silently down her face. I guess she was disappointed in us and maybe a little worried about Noe. Wanting to make her feel better, I reached over and placed my hand on her leg.

"*Mamá*, that was sure hard work. Did you and *Papá* used to work that hard out in California?"

"Yes. Why?"

"I was just wondering...*Mamá*? If we get paid for today, I think you should save the money. We don't really need to buy *cohetes*. We can just go over to the neighbors and watch them pop their *cohetes*."

Mamá gave me a little smile, wiped the tears from her cheeks, and kept driving.

Precious Moments

Teresa Barrera

The sun shone brightly as the birds chirped atop the old mesquite tree that stood in front of our home. The leaves, light green in color, slowly displayed the first signs of spring. *Abuela* and I sat under the tree on our freshly-hosed sidewalk reminiscing about "old" times. The gentle breeze slowly blew on *Abuela's* fine white, silken hair as she slowly began to share her memories. If I let myself think about that day long enough, I can still see her light up as she spoke about *Abuelo*. I can still feel the cool watermelon in my mouth, and I can still remember when she was mine.

"*Mija*, when I was a young girl we weren't allowed to have a boyfriend," *Abuela* began, as she shook her head in disagreement.

"*Los muchachos no podían venir a sacarnos de paseo.* No, they had to ask for our hand in marriage before we could ever think of going out with them," she added.

"Hand in marriage? *Wela*, are you serious?" I asked in disbelief, my eyes wide open, wanting to ask more questions.

I was sixteen at the time, so I couldn't quite understand what the big fuss about not being able to go out with a *muchacho* of your choice. I could not even fathom the thought of being betrothed to someone without even knowing him. I was quickly beginning to understand where my parents' absurd traditions and beliefs had originated.

"*Ay,* the things I did back in my days. I tell you, *solamente tu abuela lo haría,*" she stated, with a smile spreading from cheek to cheek as she remembered her rebellious days.

"A girl could get in trouble for disobeying her parents. Talking or even looking at a *muchacho* could sentence you to singlehood. A girl had to be respected and had to respect herself or else no decent guy would ever consider taking her as his wife."

With a distant look on her face, *Wela* told me stories of living the "wild life" back *en sus tiempos. Only in her time could such strictness occur,* I thought to myself. I could not even begin to imagine living the life that my grandparents had to live back on the ranch. The hardships they encountered would have been enough to literally kill me.

"*Una muchacha debía de ser rogada, no rogona.*" *Wela* quoted her *Papá,* in a deep voice, as she clinched her fist and hit her rocking chair.

"*A girl should be begged, not a beggar,*" I thought. I understood what she was trying to tell me. A guy should seek the girl and court her. In other words, girls should play hard to get.

"What do you mean?" I asked *Wela,* with curiosity written all over my face. "Does that mean you did something wrong?" I added.

"No, *mija,* but my father was born in the 1800's when prestige and family name was everything. If you dared to dishonor the name, you could be disowned," she answered with a sigh.

Abuela began to respond to my questions in a weary voice. I could tell that she was beginning to get agitated and tired. It would soon be time to take her back into our house. The doctors had told us that she couldn't be out for a long period of time for it could be detrimental to her health.

"*¿Wela, ya se quiere meter para adentro?*" I asked worriedly. I was beginning to feel tense all over; I didn't want to be the cause of a relapse. I couldn't bear the thought of seeing her hooked up to all the medical machines again.

"No, *todavía no.* I'm still not done with my story. *Pero si ya te quieres meter tú y hacer tus cosas, nos podemos meter,"* she added with a hint of hurt in her voice.

At that time, I didn't know how to feel. Should I lie to her just to take her back in? Should I let her continue the story that I so yearned to hear? *Wela* still had the desire to share her story; I was more than willing to listen. She had so many interesting stories to share. She was like a walking history book. You could ask her about almost anything in history and she had an anecdote to share with you. I wanted to hear all those stories before they were locked only in her mind forever. The first signs were already beginning to appear, and the doctors said it wouldn't be long before everything was gone. "Six months or so," they said. "That's how long she still has in her," they added.

"When I met Pedro, I was only fourteen years old," she stated, smiling as she recalled her adventure. "He had deep blue eyes in which I would get lost every time he looked at me. *¡Ése si que era un galán!"* she exclaimed as she sighed at the thought.

"*Ay, Wela,"* I said, as I chuckled at her remark. Only a person who was deeply in love could see the beauty in such things. To have loved someone with such passion, devotion, and commitment truly must have been rewarding. Now I know what she felt as she spoke of my grandfather. To have seen the greatest significance in the smallest gestures was a true sign of love.

"Pedro had been a friend of the family for many years. He often spent time with my father helping him around the ranch," Grandma explained. *"Pero cuando lo ví por primera vez, yo sabía que él sería mi esposo.* I didn't know how, but I knew that somehow the two of us would grow old together," Grandma added.

On that beautiful March day, while eating refreshing watermelons that my grandmother loved and sitting under that old mesquite tree, I learned that my grandfather was twenty-four years her senior and that my grandmother had fallen in love with him at first sight. She shared how their love at first was a secret and how they would receive love letters from one another with the aid of her two older sisters. Every Monday my two great-aunts would go to the market to wait patiently for my grandfather with his weekly love letter for my grandmother.

"*Cada lunes, como un reloj suena a tiempo, mis dos hermanas me traían las cartas de Pedro, después de su viaje al mercado.* In his letters he wrote how much he loved me and told me that he could not wait to make me his wife. *Ah, que mi Pedro,*" she sighed.

If anyone had ever found out about their secret forbidden love affair, my grandmother would have been the talk of the town. Her parents could have lost their prestigious status among the locals. Exchanging love letters or poems with men during *sus tiempos* was not common. A girl may have been considered less than worthy of a decent man if she was ever caught. However, my grandmother did not care. She was in love with this man, and she would do anything for him.

"*Un día, finalmente llegó esa carta que yo tanto añoraba,*" Grandma said with a smile on her face.

Enclosed within that letter were the words that my grandmother had long awaited to read.

"*Hoy iré a pedir tu mano para que nos puédanos casar,*" she quoted.

My grandfather was to ask for her hand in marriage that night. Within the envelope she found a gold ring. She had been right; she would get to spend the rest of her life with him.

"*Este anillo fué el que tu abuelo me mandó ese día.* I have carried this ring with me since that day," she explained.

My great-grandparents gave my grandfather their blessing for his marriage to my grandmother. Age didn't seem to matter. Although it may seem odd to hear of such an age difference between two people, love really did conquer all odds. My grandparents remained happily married until the death of my grandfather at the age of ninety-three.

Growing up I always loved hearing the story of their romance. The events that led to their engagement to this day still amaze me. The excitement and thrill of their once "forbidden love" still enlightens me. The way that their love story unfolded always held my attention. My grandmother truly defied all of society's norms.

Although my grandmother is now gone, I can still feel the gentle breeze on my face as we sat and talked under the old mesquite tree. That bright spring day when my grandmother was still mine lives in my memory.

"Fight for what you believe in, *mija*. Trust the Lord, yourself, and follow your heart, for you can never go wrong," were the last words that she told me that day.

Those precious moments spent with my grandmother will forever be etched in my mind. To this day, I live by her words of wisdom.

One in a Million
Maria Elena Betancourt

I f anyone could find a hundred and one ways of making money, it is Mother. Some of her ideas are wacky while others total failures, yet Mother manages to make and save money most people wouldn't begin to dream about.

Mother is a coupon freak. She has coupons in her purse, kitchen, dining, bed, and living rooms. I wonder how she manages to keep track of what coupons are located where, but she does. Whenever I ask her if she has a particular coupon, she goes to an anonymous pile and pulls out several. One day after noticing the piles were never ending, I asked her how she managed to accumulate so many? Her response was, *"El señor que me deja el periódico es mi amigo. El me trae todos los cupones que le sobran. Vanessa también me trae periódicos de toda la vecindad. Yo no sabía de donde los estaba trayendo, pero Don José* [her neighbor] *me vino a decir que pescó a Vanessa con su periódico. Le tuve que pagar el papel."*

I thought, *the fire marshal is going to condemn her house if he sees all of these papers, and someone is going to shoot her dog when words gets around it is the newspaper bandit. The coupons are breeding and multiplying all over her house.* My brother, Joey, throws daily fits; Mother holds her nose in the air and tells him, *"Por eso no tengo nadie que me mande."* I keep my mouth shut because I have been the recipient of many items: trash bags, toothpaste, laundry and dishwashing detergent, pampers, and groceries. The list is long.

I would be a fool to antagonize her on this subject, but my husband does not hold his tongue back. He keeps warning me in a mocking way, "If you and your mother ever go to jail for raiding stores with those coupons, don't call me!" Somehow he is still not convinced that all is legal when we wipe out stores with her coupons. Two months ago, I bought thirty boxes of trash bags. Mother bought about the same amount, and Estella bought even more. We paid ten cents per box. We had to make several trips to the store to accomplish this feat though. By the end of the trips, we were getting weird looks from the cashiers.

Mom is also a garage sale junkie. This is one hobby that drives me nuts. We have been known to stop the car in twenty-two seconds while driving fifty miles an hour because Mother saw a garage sale sign. "*Mija, ¡mira allá está una* garage sale*!*" "*Pero amá,* you don't even have your glasses, *¿cómo puedes ver tan lejos?*" "*¡Tu nomás dale!*" We know better than to argue. A few years ago, mother discovered that she had a knack for buying good quality things at cheap prices, and then reselling them at much higher prices in *her* garage sales. At her last garage sale, my sister Estella told me that Mother made over five hundred dollars in profit. Estella knows because she counted the money. Mother was quiet about the affair. Perhaps she thought that the Betancourt clan would start lining up at her door asking for money if word got out.

I usually go along with her ideas because Mother won't take no for an answer, but I drew the line at garage sales when she mentioned Houston. I know that she had been thinking about it for several days when she made the suggestion. "*Mija, he estado pensando. ¿Por qué no vamos a las* garage sales *en* Houston *un fin de semana?*" I started shaking my head. She was ready. "*Nos llevamos a los niños.*" I tried to tell her that gasoline, food, and lodging for two adults and five hungry children costs money, but she insisted. "*¿Ay cuánto se puede gastar?*" Not only that, but the thought of driving seven hours with the Ramos five seemed unbearable. Knowing that none of this was going to deter her, I decided I was going to give her a sneak preview if she kept on insisting. I thought, *an hour and* *one half drive to Brownsville with her five darling grandchildren should rid her of the notion forever. I will wear earplugs to and from.*

Another one of her not-too-bright ideas a few months ago involved me. Mother plays Bingo Wingo. One day I arrived at her house from school. She was waiting for me, *"¡Mija, nomás me falta un número para ganar el Bingo Wingo!"*

I told her, *"Amá,* there are probably a few hundred thousand other Texans saying the same thing." I swore up and down that I would not get involved in this one because I had learned a lesson the last time. "Don't even ask me to take you. *Yo sé en donde están los periódicos de ayer."* Ten minutes later, we were driving through town. I ended up driving her to just about every convenience store in Edinburg looking for the previous day's newspaper that held the winning number that every person across the state of Texas needed. To make a long story short, other people knew that the previous day's papers are thrown in the trash dumpsters outside. We didn't find any papers, but I did encounter bugs, rotting food, dirty pampers, and other paraphernalia. I was swearing under my breath the whole time. *How could I have fallen for this one? Didn't I say that I would never again be her partner in crime after the last time when she talked me into picking up discarded flowers from area cemeteries because her friend needed some, and she had found another way to make quick money? Even though she dismissed my concerns with, "Me dijeron que sí, como quiera las tiran," I had been so scared that we would be arrested for the worst sin imaginable—taking flowers from dead people, and here I was again. Don't I ever learn?* Needless to say, she did not join the ranks at the Texas newly rich. I swear that if she ever asks again, I am going to take along a step stool and let her get a firsthand look at what I saw. I told mother if she ever wins any money, she will probably have paid that amount several times over in subscription fees to the *San Antonio Light.*

Another failed scheme was the "mother" of her grand ideas. It started when her friend, Amparo, told her that people paid good money to sitters willing to take care of older citizens whose only fault was being too old to stay alone. Mother thought the idea sounded great and announced she was going to, "*buscar un anciano para cuidar y ganar mucho dinero como mi comadre Amparo.*" A week later, she proudly announced that she had found *una ancianita.*

I inquired who, why, and how much?

She accused me, "*tú todo el tiempo piensas lo peor.*" I zipped my lips. Two weeks later, the *ancianita* was taken to mother's home for the weekend. The daughter forgot to tell my mother that her mother did not sleep at night and was probably suffering from Alzheimer's. Mother said that the *ancianita* went to the bathroom about twenty times the first night. The second night, the *ancianita* forgot to tell mother that she needed to use the bathroom. Mother's eyes were watery when she recounted the previous night's drama. "She relieved herself in her clothes, found a paper towel, wiped herself, and deposited the waste in my purse. *Anduve buscando hasta que encontré de dónde venía el olor.*" Mother told me all of this on Sunday afternoon. The daughter was long overdue in picking up her mother. Mine announced that she was ready to cry. When I inquired how much she was going to earn, she said, "*No se. La señora nomás me la dejó.*" I jammed my lips shut to keep quiet. The daughter had not discussed fees with Mother in her hurry to get away. Much later, I found out that Mother had been paid twenty-five dollars for the longest weekend of her life.

These are just some of the examples of Mother's moneymaking schemes. Some backfire on her like the case with the *ancianita*, but she is usually successful. Mother was not always so smart, but like almost everyone else, she discovered her knack during desperate financial times. After Dad left, money was always tight, but we all worked to help bring in a little. After we all got married, Mother was left with the sudden realization that she was on her own. Faced with no job, very little education, no car, and no one to turn to for financial assistance, Mother knew that it was either sink or swim. She swam fast and hard. Now we all joke that Mother probably makes more money from her coupon refunding and garage sales than we all do working full time. She is quite a character.

Tres Mojaditos
Evaristo Bocanegra

At seven when the
last melon crate has been packed,
the stifling stuffy *bodega* sets them free.
They'll meet at a bar on 17th street.

There in the darkness sharing
Rosa, *la cantinera*,
and a round of
cool soothing *cervezitas*,

Sit Chemo, El Indio,
and Rey, puffing,
laughing, drinking
their lives away.

They feed the
Spanish juke box
that sings all
through the night

About a lost love,
*"Si tú supieras
cómo sufro
por tus besos."*

Oblivious and numb,
happy to erase
the pain and grief
of yesterday,

They gain new courage.
Chingones! prouder
as the spirits rise
and the music gets louder,

They growl and yell
gritos de alegría, wild tigers
daring all to put out
their raging fires.

But no one listens.
What good to subdue
three poor drunken fools?
So they'll sink deep in their stools

'Til the morning sun arrives
melts their bravado and rage,
drives them back to reality
to toil in a galvanized cage.

Sometimes

Veronica Casas

Sometimes we remember how things used to be.
When see a back street alley or hear a song on the radio,
we remember what we were thinking, what we were feeling,
even what we did.

Sometimes we remember good things, sometimes bad.
Mostly we remember loved ones,
many times bringing tears to our eyes.

Sometimes we close our eyes and go back
even for a brief time
to see the wonderful times that are long gone.
Or are they?

God gave us a gift,
so we could go on.

We can live in the now that He has blessed us with,
and we can live in the then whenever our hearts desire.

My *Abuelita's* Legacy
Elvia C. Cavazos

S outh of the border, down a dirt road in a ramshackle hut lived a frail old lady. She dressed in simple clothes and covered her hair with a solemn-black laced veil as if to hide her lost youth. We tenderly called this old lady *Abuelita*. We spent at least one Saturday every month with her. Our family would pile like packed sardines into our family station wagon to make this pilgrimage. My dad, who was extremely fond of his mother-in-law, would coach us on exactly what to say and how to treat her. "Remember, *le besan la mano,*" my father would say. We never complained; we didn't mind kissing her gnarled hands, a customary display of reverence. Looking back I can see that *Abuelita* has molded me into the person I have become.

She mystified me. When you looked into her eyes, you could see that deep inside she held secrets. Her dark thin hands, worn and weathered, told a story, a story of hard work and pain. You see, *Abuelita* became a widow very young. She struggled to raise all her children on her own, performing odd jobs. By day she tended a store; by night she washed and ironed for well-to-do families. She was a single mother in a time when being a single mother was a death sentence. Many suitors asked for her hand, yet she chose to raise her four children on her own. Looking at her now you would not know she once was a beautiful woman. That time has passed for her.

An independent lady, she never took a handout in her life, instead she worked from dusk to dawn to survive in a cruel world made only for men. *Mi viejita*, as my mother called her, was a symbol of strength and determination. I always wanted to emulate her, and I truly believe that some of her characteristics rubbed off on me or at least my mother always said I was as *terca* or as stubborn as my grandmother. This characteristic helped me survive when I went back to school to get a college education after my third child's birth. I felt rejuvenated, as if I was given a second chance in life. Possibly the force that drove *Abuelita* to create a better life for her children was the same force that motivated me to further my education so I could do the same for my own children.

Though I realized that returning to college after so many years was going to be hard, I truly did not have a clue how difficult it would be. I remember signing up for eighteen to twenty-one hours a semester. My family and friends told me I was crazy, out of my mind. They advised me to take it easy. "You'll dig your own grave," they said. Everybody else knew what I knew deep inside of me but would never admit. It would be deadly to take this load and be a mother of three, and more importantly, a mother of a newborn.

As anybody who has been a parent knows, the first year of your child's life you do not sleep at all. But I was determined, and drawing strength from my *Abuelita*, I had resolved to walk across the platform and receive that college degree. Nothing existed from sunup to sundown but my family and education. Even though I longed to be a sleeping beauty during this period of my life, I remained focused, and I graduated.

I hope and pray that the Lord blesses me with many years as he blessed *Abuelita*. And when my hair turns gray and my hands become gnarled, I wish to inspire my children and their children to work hard to achieve their goals. My prayer is that as I grow old, my children's children will revere me in the same way I revered *Abuelita*.

Vida En El Barrio
Jesús A. Chávez

Growing up in the *barrio*, contrary to what others might think, was great. In my mind I'm still there. *"¡Jesús, levántate!"* my mother would say. I didn't want to get up. I would always go to bed late. My mom was in the kitchen making breakfast. *Las tortillas recién hechas*, mmm..., what an aroma. I have yet to smell any aroma as good as my mom's *tortillas*. *"¡Ándale apúrale!"* she would yell. If I didn't hurry, I wouldn't get to eat breakfast.

After breakfast I had to walk to school. I didn't mind because everyone in the *barrio* would walk together. As I was getting ready, I could hear my friend, Toño, calling me, *"Órale Chuy apúrale vamos a estar* late." He just hated getting late to school. I don't remember when it happened, but it happened. Some of my friends got bicycles, but we didn't think it was cool to ride a bike to school.

Sometimes when we would get to school, we had a little time before class. Everyone just walked around. Teachers hated that. They wanted us to sit in front of our classroom. We hated that.

One teacher that I remember in particular was Mr. Ricky. His real name was Mr. Andrés Ricardo. Anytime he heard us talking Spanish he would admonish, "Speak English." I hated when he told us that. Not that I didn't know how to speak English, but I felt pride in my Spanish language.

Every time he would say that I would respond, "Okay, Mr.

Ricky." I can still remember his face when he heard me say that. It was as if he had just sat on a pin. His eyebrows would arch and his forehead would wrinkle. The funny part was that no more words would come out of his mouth, yet I knew this upset him. I just didn't know why he kept on insisting. After a while I got fed up and started ignoring him.

One day as Toño and I were passing by, Toño told me, "*Tengo sueño, era muy tarde anoche cuando nos metimos.*"

"Boys, remember, please speak English. You're in school now and we need to follow this rule." Mr. Ricardo said as he passed by.

"*¿Tienes sueño? Si nomás te metiste y te dormiste. Ni siquiera te bañaste anoche. Te puedo oler,*" I said laughing.

I was just kidding, but I said it in Spanish so Mr. Ricardo would realize that I was ignoring him. That's when I got in real trouble and was sent to the office. It didn't matter because this was my language. The way we spoke in our home, our *barrio*. I was not trying to act smart. I was trying to make a point. My language, as long as we were not in class, was my choice. I was not saying any bad words. That would have changed the purpose.

Walking home after school was something special. Everyone from the *barrio* would walk home together. Nobody rode the bus or got picked up by their parents. This was our time to *platicar* without any adults around. Sometimes I would call out to Veronica, "*Espérame para ir contigo.*" Toño knew I liked her, but we were such good friends, I couldn't tell her. I enjoyed just talking to her. Everyone would be talking to each other, so she never realized how much I liked her.

Crossing the railroad tracks was kind of peculiar. Now as I look back, it is clear to me that I realized we were home. *El barrio* was my home. I could hear the sounds of our music. My mom was always listening to KGBT, her radio station. My older brother and his friends would be listening to Ricky Smith *y La Movida*, his favorite group. Everyone outside was playing, talking, listening to music, just having a good time.

As I walked into my house, my mom's cooking could be appreciated. She made the best *mole y arroz con pollo*. She would tell me, *"Cámbiate y lávate las manos para que comas."* Since we had school clothes and house clothes, we had to change before eating.

When we were done eating, my night was just getting started. I would go outside with my friends and just hang around.

I can still hear the sounds of *mi barrio*. In my mind, kids will always be playing in the streets, listening to music, and just walking around talking. *La vida en el barrio, qué sabrosa.*

If I were to live again, I wouldn't want to live anywhere else.

Mi Desierto
Miguel Chuca

The sun was giving up its light, and I could see the desert's dirt become a reddish color. It felt as if I had never seen this miracle happen even though I had watched it for the past sixteen years, and I knew that it would be a long time before I would ever see this again. Mother Nature created this view on the west side of Texas around El Paso.

"You know what, *Mamá*? I'm leaving for school, for college, and I'm going to go run track and cross-country for the University of Texas-Pan American! The coach has offered me a full scholarship!"

My mother wasn't the type of person who was going to hold me down. She had taught me to think for myself, to dream, to go out there in life and become someone. She wanted me to get an education, even if it meant that she would lose her baby boy. I am the youngest boy in a family of two older brothers and two younger sisters. *"Tu eres mi baby, mijo,* even when you are all grown up you will always be my baby," *Mamá* would always say.

Mamá and I were close, and as I think about it now, I know why. Right from the start, before I even turned a month old, I became sick. My parents lived in East Los Angeles where *Papá* could find work. I ended up in the hospital where the doctors didn't think I'd survive, yet mother never faltered in her faith.

My parents moved back to El Paso, where they once lived, right after I was released from the hospital. I was about one-year old. I don't remember any of this, but my mother and family often tell and retell this story.

As I packed for college, I packed memories too.

"It's time to go, *mijo*. We were able to rent a car because your *Tío* Shorty lent us his credit card, so I want you to call him before we leave and thank him. You know that everyone from the family is proud of you because you are the first one to ever go to college."

It was time for me to leave *Mi Desierto*, my hometown. We began the twelve-hour drive to my new home. I was driving a small red rented car, packed to the gunnels with my things, *Mamá*, *Papá*, my five-year old sister, and my friend, Adrian.

As I was driving to Edinburg, I thought of all the things that I had gone through with *Mamá*. During my first five-month hospital stay, she would leave the house at 8:00 A.M., take the one-hour trip to the hospital, and be with me all day. Sometimes she stayed all night. It is unbelievable that as a child I went three more times to the hospital. *Mamá* did not leave me, not one single time did she leave me. She stayed there with me day and night. Once when there were nurses all around giving me shots, she held my hand tightly and did not leave my sight. All I could think about as I drove along was, "If I die today, I know that I was loved very much in this world."

"Look Out! *¡Aguas con el Venado! ¡Trucha!*" Adrian yelled. I was so busy recalling memories, I didn't notice a monstrous deer with antlers big enough to pick up our petite car and body slam it into the ground! I jammed on the brakes. My *papá* and *mamá* woke up to see a deer standing right in the highway just a few inches away from the car. The deer finally moved away from the road and *Papá* took over the wheel. I fell into a fitful sleep of deer, and hospitals, and shots.

When I woke up, we had arrived in Edinburg. The day passed quickly and soon it was time for my parents to leave. I hugged everyone and tried to hold my tears. When it was time to say goodbye to my mother I asked, *"Mamá,* do you remember the songs that I would play in my room? I want to give you this song from *el grupo Maná,* it's called *El Desierto.* It's my gift to you for always being there for me, and I promise you that I will not let you down."

Ya me voy muy lejos del pueblo, empacando maletas aguardando recuerdos de amor...... Ya me voy hacia el norte, dejo novias, mis calles, mi gente, mi México... ay ay ay... algún día yo volveré... ay ay ay te prometo mi amor... no lloraré mientras camino... el desierto y la luna... se vienen conmigo...

Las Mañanitas
Isabel Corona

"Eva, wake up *mija!* Eva! It's time to get up!"

"*Sí, Mami. ¡Ya voy!*"

Eva sits up, turns, places her feet on the floor and pushes herself up in one smooth motion.

"*Ya voy Mami. ¿Mami?*" Slowly Eva stops. Mami is not here. (Mami will not be here today or tomorrow or ever.)

Eva turns and goes back to bed. "*Today is my birthday,*" she thinks, "*will anyone remember? Today I am eleven years old. I am almost a teenager.*"

The blankets welcome her in. She is not ready to get up; it's too early.

María turns over in her sleep on her side of the bed but doesn't wake up.

"*¿Mami, donde estás?*

Mamá why did you have to leave?

Sin tí, nobody cares.

All I hear is, '*¡Estás chiflada! Mami te tenía muy chiflada.*' (Is it my fault that Mami loved me? Is it my fault that she left?)

Eva knows that November 3, 1971 is just another day to her sisters. Papi never remembers any of his children's birthdays.

"Get up María, Eva, it's time to go to school," Lupita calls as she opens the bedroom door. "Eva, María, it's almost seven. You are going to miss the bus."

María mumbles something in her sleep, but otherwise she doesn't move. Eva gets out of bed and plods to the bathroom.

"I knew that they would not remember my birthday, I just knew it!" Eva glowers at her reflection and quickly brushes her teeth.

I know that Mami would have remembered that today is my birthday.

Knock, knock. "Hurry Eva, I need to use the bathroom," María yells through the door.

"Okay, I'm almost finished." Eva combs her hair and opens the door. "I'll wait for you at the bus stop, María. Don't be late!"

"Here is your lunch, Eva. I will be working when you get home from school. Remember this is your week to sweep the house."

"Yes, I know, Lupe."

"María, hurry up, Eva's leaving for the bus stop. You're going to miss the bus again, and I am not taking you to school!"

"I'm coming. I'm almost ready," María answers.

Eva turns and walks out the door. *"Just like yesterday! Mami, can you see me today? Do you know what today is?"*

The walk to the corner is so long. Eva turns and looks back at her house. The sun peeks shyly over the roof. The front porch is in deep shadows, waiting for the first glimpse of morning. The picture window centered between the narrow side windows allows a view into the front yard, edged in the pink, yellow, and red roses that Mami loved. The honeysuckle growing wild on the fence reaches out to grab a corner of the house as if to conquer it. The mesquite stands tall and straight in the middle of the yard.

Eva squints her eyes and sees a figure standing by the door. *"¿Mami? No, it's not her. Mami will not be by the door this morning or tomorrow or ever."*

"I better get to the bus stop," she mutters to herself.

María slams the door and yells, "Wait for me, Eva. I see you! Slow down, I'm almost there." María hitches up her purse, throws dignity to the wind, and trots slowly and clumsily in her platform shoes to Eva.

"Why do you make me run? Can't you see that my shoes are starting to get unglued on this side?"

"Then don't wear them. Wear the *tenis* shoes that Lupe bought you when school started."

"*Tenis* shoes don't go with this skirt I made in Home Ec."

"Yes, they do; all the girls are wearing skirts with *tenis* shoes."

"Well, I want to wear these platform shoes. I bought them with my own money. Why shouldn't I wear them?"

Eva sighs saying, "It's not that. If they are coming unglued maybe you should ask Papi to fix them."

"Papi will just say, '*¿Qué tánto pagaste por estas cosas? Yo los puedo hacer.*' He always says that he could do something better or cheaper, but he never does it."

A cluta, clute, clute sound stirs the trees next to them.

"Look, here comes the bus. Maybe we will get a seat today. I hate being the last stop."

The dirt covered yellow and black box grinds to a stop next to them and the doors open.

"Whew! It stinks in here! When are they going to fix this bus? Look there is an empty seat. I'm glad we don't have to stand so all the boys can stare at us but not get up to give us a seat. María, I want to sit by the window."

María lets Eva slide in first and then sits down next to her. Eva stares out the window. There is *Señor* Sánchez taking the trash can to the curb and *Señora* Sánchez working on her flowers. Look, Señor Banda is piling his truck with *costales* in preparation for a day packing onions. *Señora* Chita is sitting on her porch drinking a cup of coffee. Eva slowly waves her hand in response to *Señora* Chita's wave.

Spot is running after the bus barking. "Go home!" I yell at our crazy dog.

Eva leans her head on the window and closes her eyes.

The story continues...

Mañana
Melodie Cuate

T he shrill, staccato cry of a rooster perched on a fence post announced morning had officially arrived in the South Texas countryside. Tempted by sounds of movement in the small frame home, a white dog with black spots crawled out from beneath a porch. He sat near the front door, sniffing and scratching, sniffing and scratching.

The drafty, tin-roofed house had once been white. Now the paint has peeled away from the façade almost in the same way a snake sheds its skin. The small old home was too tight a fit for the eleven family members that dwelled within. A matchbox-sized kitchen and two small bedrooms shifted and stretched out of shape with the growing family. The boys slept in one room, the girls in the other. A fourth room, the parents' bedroom, served as a family room as well.

If it were possible to get a bird's eye view of exactly where this house was located, then a bird would see that it perched on the very edge of a *monte*. To the north of this humble home, and reaching out for miles and miles, was nothing but mesquite trees, brush, cactus, brown earth, and a few lonely cattle searching for patches of fresh grass. It was a land where whitetail deer, javalina, bobcats, and coyotes thrived. To the south were open fields that eventually led to a road that was swallowed up by the horizon. The house was almost an island protecting the isolated family from an outside world.

The nearest town was McCook, a small farming community consisting of a family store located on the corner of a single intersection. Just down the road was an elementary school. Even farther south stood a Catholic Church. Acres and acres of land separated the hundred or so neighbors from each other.

Without a sound, the screen door cracked open. Metal mesh pulling loose from a bottom corner was torn and bent out of shape. A small dark-haired boy grinned at the dog whispering, "*¿Tienes hambre, Palomo?* If you want to come in, you must be very, very quiet."

The dog's tail whapped in a steady beat against the wooden door frame. He hesitated before putting on paw down inside the house; he had never been allowed there before. The young boy nodded in approval and petted the furry head enthusiastically. "*Ven páca, perrito.* Hurry before they see you."

"Tonio, don't you dare let that smelly old dog in the house," scolded Belinda, one of the little boy's sisters. "*Amá*, Tonio's letting the dog in!" She shot him a scalding look just before she rushed through the doorway of the girls' room to finish getting ready for school.

Tonio sadly closed the door on his best friend. A whimpering sound on the other side of the screen reflected what the five-year-old was feeling. He stared down at his bare feet, lonely in a home overflowing with nine children.

The voices of the family blended together weaving in and out like musical sounds of violins playing in a *corrido*.

"*Amá*, tell Luis to hurry up!"

"Where's my library book?"

"Give me back the brush."

"Adela, get up. You'll be late."

"Who tied these knots in my shoelaces?"

Tonio's smile held a secret about the shoelaces. *That's what you get for saying mean things to me,* he thought to himself.

A woman's voice called out, *"Tonio, ¿quieres almorzar?"*

"Ahi voy, Amá." The boy darted to the kitchen. He patiently watched his mother drop a single bologna sandwich in each of the brown paper bags and lunch boxes lined up on the counter as if on an assembly line. Each bag was rolled up tightly from the top. Stooping over to push aside an overflowing laundry basket, she sighed thinking about the long day ahead of her. Reaching up, she took out a bowl from the cabinet, and then sprinkled a meager portion of cornflakes in the bottom. Next, she poured milk fresh from the family cow on the cereal and placed it on the table, setting a spoon beside it. *"Aquí, mijo."*

Grabbing the spoon hungrily, he scooped up the cereal crunching loudly while he ate. "Can I go to school today?" he asked with a full mouth.

"Mijo, if you go to school, who would keep me company all day?" his *mamá* questioned.

Tonio tossed his spoon on the table and pouted, wrinkling his eyebrows together. "Ochie will be here with you," he replied sullenly.

"Ochie is only a baby. I need a man to help me with things around the house. Remember, your father has already gone to work on the tractor."

"Please, *Amá,* please," he begged.

His mother cast him a weary glance. *"Está bien, mijo.* I'll make an extra sandwich. You can pretend to go to school."

Tonio sat quietly considering what his mother had offered. He didn't understand how he could pretend to go to school. That's not what he wanted. When the bus arrived, he planned on getting in it.

His mother made one more bologna sandwich, placed it in a broken lunchbox, and set it on the table next to her youngest son. The outside of the lunchbox had a blue and red plaid design. Tonio ran his finger along the overlapping squares and rectangles. Blue was his favorite color. Most of the edges were rusty and dented, but the hinge closing the lid was intact. A cracked handle would have to be held carefully.

With the momentum of a small tornado, a large group of school-aged children filled with energy descended upon the kitchen, picking up lunches and hugging *Mamá* goodbye. Everyone was talking at once, everyone except Tonio. He knew the school bus was on its way, and he hadn't even finished his breakfast. Quickly, gobbling up a few more bites of cereal, he grabbed his lunch box and followed his sisters and brothers out the front door.

The screen door opened once again. Out rushed the children, one at a time, with Tonio trailing the others. Palomo fell in line behind Tonio. The line resembled the tail of a kite meandering back and forth through the front yard.

Arms full of schoolbooks and lunches, they followed a dirt path to the road. Without being told, the older girls made certain the younger children didn't venture too far away. They were in the habit of caring for their younger siblings. Tonio stood aside from his family, keeping watch for the bus while the others chatted happily with each other. He wanted to be the first in line.

When the long yellow vehicle finally stretched into view, he shouted out enthusiastically, "*¡Ahi viene el bus!* It's coming! It's coming!"

Felipa, another sister, took hold of his arm as the bus screeched to a halt. The door squeaked open just before the children boarded in single file, pushing Tonio to the rear of the line. After anxiously waiting his turn, the little boy eagerly took his first step into the bus. He thought to himself, *It's so big. I wonder where they want me to sit?*

His sister turned around. "Tonio, you're not old enough to go to school. You're still a baby," she said in a teasing voice. "Go back to the house before the bus driver gets angry!"

Tonio peeked around his sister at a large man with a grouchy expression sitting behind the steering wheel. He stared at the small boy and stated in a deep, intimidating voice, "Hurry up, children."

Tonio jumped back. The bus driver frightened him. Maybe his sister was right. He didn't want that Anglo man yelling at him. Holding his lunch box tightly, he slowly turned around and stepped off the bus. The door slammed so abruptly, he jumped back a second time.

Staring up into the windows, at the happy expressions of the children, Tonio's brown eyes shone with unshed tears. His chance to go to school was gone. He kicked at a clod of dirt with his bare toes, sending it flying into the side of the bus and crumbling on impact.

Luis, his brother, laughed and pointed down at him from an open window while the school bus pulled away. "Just wait till you get home!" Tonio shouted angrily. "I'll tie your shoelaces in a zillion knots this time!"

The boy shaded his eyes from the sun as the bus carrying his brothers and sisters became smaller and smaller, finally vanishing behind fields of rust colored grain waving in a southwestern breeze. A lone tear inched its way down his cheek. Palomo rubbed his wet nose on Tonio's arm. Resting his hand on the dog's back, he looked up and followed the flight of two white wing doves crisscrossing a yellow sky. Their shadowy silhouettes made him smile. *"Vente,* Palomo. Let's go hunting. I'll go to school *mañana."*

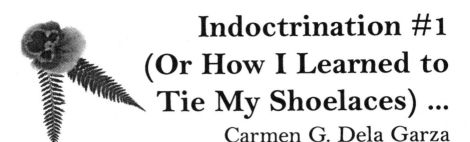

Indoctrination #1 (Or How I Learned to Tie My Shoelaces) ...

Carmen G. Dela Garza

"**C**lose your eyes and think of a memory from your childhood," bids our professor in her lilting, sedating voice. Surrendering to her invitation, my eyes slowly flutter then shut. Panoramas of thoughts tumble through my head: an impending hurricane, end- of-the-month bills, the start of school looming, my last of four sons about to start high school. Flashes of childhood memories start taking shape. Relinquishing the present, succumbing to the past, I embark on a journey that will take me back approximately forty-four years to the age of six. Etched in the depository of a long-ago memory, I am contentedly starting my first day of first grade at Immaculate Conception School.

For years *ad infinitum*, the first grade teacher had been Sister Mary Alexis--kindly and old. Looking forward to having her as my teacher, I would continue the tradition of being the third Garcia sister to be taught by Sister Mary Alexis. However, this was not meant to be. She had retired that summer, so our first grade class would be starting out with a brand new teacher--Sister Mary Javier. Young and Hispanic, she was an anomaly at Immaculate Conception School; all the other Sisters were old and Irish. Wouldn't you know that this would be our first-grade teacher's first year teaching first graders!

Traveling from our *pueblito* of Rio Grande City to the big city of McAllen just to buy my school clothes only added to the excitement of starting school. Recalling that first day, my mother dressed me up in brand new clothes bought at Sears. Brand new saddle oxford shoes complemented the clothes. Completing the ensemble was a brand new school satchel made of plaid material. Brand new #2 real wood pencils bulged from its plastic pouch. Vibrant Crayola crayons waited to make their debut. Notebook paper clamored to become the vehicles of my imagination. Delightedly, I sat in the back seat of my parents' Ford absorbing the intoxicating smells of the newness of everything. Butterflies danced in my stomach as first grade made its imminent arrival!

Chachalacas heralded the day! Living across the street from the Catholic school and church, I set off alone. Even now, I can see my mother watching me from behind the hurricane fence of our home as I crossed the street, taking care to look both ways. Entering the first-grade classroom with my classmates, we faced Sister Mary Javier who greeted us sternly. Not dissuaded by the severity of her demeanor, I thought, *What a comfort to see a Sister who looks like the rest of us—brown eyes and olive skin.* Already acquiring a writer's keen eye for observation, I did detect a wisp of brown hair escaping from behind the white habit that framed her face.

Unlike the first-grade teachers of today who have been trained to welcome their little ones in a nurturing and loving way, Sister Mary Javier began at once to mold and shape us. "No time to tarry," she chided. "Idleness is the devil's workshop," she reminded us. Feeling confident and optimistic coupled with a desire to please, I quickly chose a desk at the front of the classroom. Hadn't my favorite board game always been "Go to the Head of the Class"? (I was always the teacher.) In no time, the big brass bell rang and it was recess! My little *comadritas*—Luisa, Cecilia, Odilia, Judy, and Vangie and I—cavorted on the monkey bars, swung on the giant swings, slid on the slippery slide. My shoelaces came undone. Untied? Unfastened? Loosened?

Running in from recess, I stopped as Sister Mary Javier commanded, "Maria del Carmen," her voice cold, her face dour, "tie your shoelaces." Without a moment's hesitation, I immediately and obediently bent to tie them. Suddenly realizing that I hadn't been taught to tie my shoelaces, I felt a rush of embarrassment shoot through my body. Being *la consentida* of the family, the youngest of the three girls and a baby born late in life to my parents, my mother had always coddled me by snapping snaps, buttoning buttons, braiding hair, and yes, sadly, tying shoelaces.

Helplessly I looked down at my shoelaces. Shamefully I looked up at Sister. Judgmentally she glared. "Well, what are you waiting for?" She demanded to know. I stammered. "I...I don't know how to tie my shoelaces, Sister."

Sister Mary Javier ordered, "Go home and learn to tie your shoelaces, Maria del Carmen. Do not return to school until you have learned." I somehow stumbled out of the classroom and back to my mother's bedroom.

On that September afternoon, in the sanctuary of my home, amid the stinging of my hot tears and the shattering of my six-year old self-esteem, my mother loving and calmly bent over to teach me how to tie my shoelaces. "You loop, place your thumb here, loop over the thumb, remove the thumb quickly, and tie" "Now, do it again, *mijita*." Feverishly, as if on a mission, I practiced innumerable times the seemingly innocuous art of shoelace tying. Finally achieving the knack for it, my mother then made me walk back to school so I could finish the first day successfully. She, knowingly or unknowingly, taught me another valuable lesson that later in life would come in handy when the calamities of life seemed unbearable to face. Little did I know that this lesson was just the beginning of my Catholic school indoctrination.

Fast-forward to August 1985. Twenty-four years have slipped by. Now thirty-years old, I have just given birth to our third son while my first-born son, Danny, four-years-old, looks forward to his first day of Pre-Kinder. Driving him to the big city of McAllen, we buy his clothes at a familiar department store. Complementing his ensemble is not the plaid school satchel of yesteryear, but the ubiquitous backpack made of mesh material—this is a gift from my mother, now sixty-eight years old. She and my father still live in the same *pueblito*, in the same house they've lived in since 1945. His paternal grandma supplied him with the other necessary accouterments of pre-school education—the vibrant Crayola crayons, the #2 pencils, the notebook paper. However, there's one thing missing from Danny's ensemble—saddle oxfords. Instead, Danny sports a pair of sneakers that have come equipped with none other than that state-of-the-art marvel--VELCRO!

Family Secrets and Final Goodbyes

Laura Liza Escobedo

Steel gray drapes block out the brightness of the morning sun making the shadowy room dismal and oppressive. Light--a single hazy stream, shines through where the curtains meet. The sparse décor consists of a wrought-iron bed, a beaded rosary hanging from the bedpost, a nightstand covered with small medicine bottles, and a tall glass candle in front of a picture of the Virgin Mary holding Baby Jesus, a prayer to the Blessed Mother fastened on its back. Sitting at the end of the bed is an antique chest; a plaid wing chair rests by the night-stand. Lying on the bed, covered up to her neck in a frayed and faded yellow and blue quilted blanket, is a woman with white hair so insignificant it can't hide the dark patches of her head. Her pale face resembles a map with hundreds of lines where ice-blue veins stand out like rivers. Cracked, bloodless lips part slightly as the woman tries to breathe.

Deep in sleep, the woman sees a young girl of fourteen with glorious red hair, rosy red lips, and eyes like brown velvet. The woman recognizes the happy and carefree girl as Leticia who attends Immaculate Conception; Leticia expresses great excitement at the thought of graduating the same day as her birthday, May 28th. Her mother said she could have a *quinceañera* if her grades were exceptional, and they were. Coming home from school with visions of the party dress her mom will make for her, she walks oblivious to the humidity draping around her. Leticia imagines her mother using the emerald green taffeta she has purchased recently to accent the traditional soft white of the bodice. After all, that shade of green, her favorite, perfectly complements her coloring and will show off her hair beautifully. Preoccupied in her thoughts, she fails to see the truck dogging her, but the old woman sees the dusty old black pick-up truck with a bronzed *hombre* sitting behind the wheel. Slick midnight hair pokes out from under his well-worn straw hat. Thick lashed liquid gold eyes remind the woman of a large black panther. Pencil thin moustache whiskers above thick lips conceal white teeth. Slowing down, the black truck draws nearer, pulling up to Leticia at the corner.

"Hey, *Chiquita*, can you help me? I'm lost."

Thinking of only her *quinceañera*, happy-go-lucky Leticia doesn't seem to hear.

Again he shouts, "Hey, *mijita*, can you please help me?"

Leticia turns and smiles, "Sorry, are you talking to me?" She stops cautiously. Resting his tanned weathered elbow on the door, his snakelike eyes take in her sweetness.

Shining his best smile, he greets the budding adolescent girl. "*Hola*, can you help me? I'm new here, and I can't find the sheriff's office. I just got hired—you're looking at the newly appointed deputy sheriff," he boasts. "I'm sorry I'm being rude. I'm Ramiro and you are...?"

Blushing, she answers innocently, "Leticia." Looking down at her black buckle shoes, "Nice to meet you, *Señor*."

"*Por favor*, call me Ramiro; I will be offended if you don't."

Pointing north, Leticia tells him, "The sheriff's office is in the courthouse; you can't miss it, *Señor*— I mean Ramiro." Smiling shyly, she adds, "You go two blocks north, then you turn left on Main Street; it's halfway down the block. It's the tallest building."

Ramiro replies in mock confusion, "Okay, I go north a few blocks until I hit Mainly Road. I'll see the building at the end of the block. *¿sí?*"

Exasperated, Leticia says, "No, No, No, that's not what I said.

You go north till you hit Main Street, turn left, you can't miss it!"

Feigning confusion Ramiro asks, "Wouldn't it be easier if you just showed me?"

Shaking her head, Leticia replies, "I'm sorry, but I can't. I'm not allowed to talk to strangers. I shouldn't even be talking to you."

Looking hurt, Ramiro says, "I'm not a stranger. I told you I'm the new deputy sheriff. Doesn't that mean that you can trust me?"

Leticia, unsure, whispers, "Well, yes, I guess so."

Smiling, Ramiro says, "So see, you can trust me, no? After all, the sheriff hired me to put bad *hombres* behind bars. Doesn't that make me a good guy?"

Biting down on her lip, Leticia answers, "I guess you're right."

Ramiro, a black snake keen upon his prey, declares, "Well that settles it. Hop in. You can show me the way to the courthouse then I'll take you home, *¿sí?*"

Leticia nervously walks around to the passenger door and slowly gets in. Ramiro, a sly smile on his face, puts all his weight onto the gas pedal and peels off.

***

As the man enters the room, he hears the labored wheezing of the old woman. He stands next to her bed and makes the sign of the cross. "In the name of the Father, the Son, and the Holy Spirit." He reaches down and makes the same sign on the woman's forehead. Slowly he picks up her cold, limp, wrinkled hand, and holds it in his warm, firm grip. Eyes closed, face raised, the man prays, "Our Father who art in heaven...Amen." He turns and pulls the chair close to the bed and lowers himself into its lumpy softness. He softly whispers, "I'm here now. Can you hear me?"

White chapped lips move.

The man leans closer, "Everything is going to be fine. Are you cold? How are you feeling?" Strong hands pick up a beige flannel blanket, placing the frayed fuzziness over the quilt which already covers her body. "There's a draft in here. I feel quite chilly myself, although the day is glorious outside."

The white lips ask softly, so softly, that he barely hears her, "Charles, is that you?"

Squeezing her hand, "Yes, Sweetheart. I have come to visit you, to check on how you are feeling."

Dark foggy eyes open. "My time nears."

Tears well in his eyes. "I know, Dear Heart, but you must rest, and try not to overdo."

"I wish I was beautiful again. You do remember, Charles?"

"You're still beautiful!"

"Oh, Charles, is that why you married me?"

"I fell in love with you the first time I laid eyes on you. You looked so beautiful yet frightened, almost as if you were an angel who lost her halo. All I could think about was how I was going to protect you. I knew then that I wanted to marry you."

Coughing, the woman says, "Charles, I have something to tell you."

"Here drink this; it will help you rest."

"No-oo, I must talk to you. Please, Charles."

Turning away, he dries his eyes with his handkerchief. "It's almost time for lunch. Try to rest while I go check on it."

The medication begins to work, and once again the woman falls into a deep, but labored sleep.

***

"Oh no, Ramiro, you missed the turn. Didn't you hear me? I told you that was it."

"That's okay. We'll just take the long way."

Leticia looks around, "I don't think that's such a good idea. It's getting late and my mom is going to be worried."

"It's not that late. Why don't you just calm down?"

Fidgeting, Leticia says, "Maybe you could stop? I could call home to let *Mamá* know that I'm running late."

"*No haye necesídad.*"

In desperation Leticia pleads, "Please stop! You're scaring me. I want to go home. Besides this isn't the way to the courthouse.

"*Yo sé Chiquita.*"

Sensing danger, Leticia starts to cry. Leticia begs, "Please Mister Ramiro, the joke is over. Please take me home!"

"I intend to *Querida.*"

"Where are you taking me? This isn't the way to my house!"

"*Tenga paciencia, Querida.*"

Frightened she replies, "Please don't call me that. My name is Leticia."

"Such a pretty name for a pretty girl."

Leticia threatens, "If you don't stop this truck, I'll jump!"

With that, Ramiro gives her a back-handed slap, dazing the girl. Blood drips from her cheek where his ring made contact and broke the baby-soft skin. A bruise begins.

"No one threatens me! *¡Nadie!* Do you understand?"

In tears, she whispers, "Yes."

***

Although the sun is directly overhead the room still feels damp. The woman begins to cough as the door opens and Charles comes in carrying a tray.

"I've returned, Love, and I've brought you some wonderful *caldito de pollo.*" Charles places the tray on the night stand and helps the woman sit by fluffing up her pillows. The woman, eyes red, turns to face him, "Love, I just can't. I haven't the strength."

"Sure you can, Sweetheart. Come on. The consommé will make you feel so much better."

"For you, I guess I can try."

"That's my girl."

Swallowing a couple of spoonfuls the woman begins to choke. The loving husband offers his frail wife some warm *té de manzanilla.*

"Here try some of this." Sipping slowly, the woman's coughing ceases. Weakly, she says, "Dear Charles, please don't let me die before making things right between us. I couldn't bear to die with the guilt."

"Things are fine between us, Love. You know that. Besides I plan to have you around for a while yet."

"No, Charles, I've kept something from you!"

"Hush, you need to rest. No sense in wasting energy. I'm going to leave now, and I'll see you in a few hours. You will be here when I get back, won't you?"

"Yes, my sweet Charles, I'll be here."

Slowly Charles turns away. Opening the door, he takes another look at the woman he loves. Tears spill down his weathered face; he quietly closes the door.

***

A blindingly bright light fills the stark white room. Leticia stirs on a single hard bed, she is racked with pain and confusion.

"It hurts, Amá, it hurts! Please Amá, make it go away! I hate that smell. Take it away, Amá, take it away! Just make it stop!"

"Doctor, the patient is responding to the smelling salts, but she seems disoriented."

"It's a wonder she's alive. She's had a traumatic experience, and she may wish she had died when she recovers. Have the parents been notified?"

"Yes, Doctor. The mother is waiting in the hall."

"What about her father?"

"He passed away a few years ago."

"Well, there's no putting it off. I'll go outside to see her mother. Don't leave her. She may awaken to full consciousness any minute."

"Yes, Doctor."

The woman in the hall screams, "No! It can't be. Not my Letty! She's not yet fifteen for God's sake! No! Please, not my Letty." "¡Ay, Dios mío, ayúdame!"

***

The sun has set. Charles walks back into the room and lights a candle. He kneels and bows his head in prayer, "Hail Mary, full of Grace, the Lord is with Thee, Blessed are Thou...Amen." The man prays fervently in silence.

"Charles, how long have you been kneeling there? You know your knees can't take the strain."

"Not long."

"Charles, do you remember the day we met?"

The man wistfully smiles, "Yes, it was the most wonderful day in my life. A day I treasure more than any other."

"No regrets?"

"None! Why do you ask?"

"Don't you remember that was the day you decided you were no longer going into the priesthood?"

"Ah, yes, but still have no regrets. You are part of me. Besides, I have always believed that the Lord intervened where you and I were concerned."

"Really, Charles?"

"Yes, how else would I have met the perfect woman for me?"

"But I wasn't a woman, not in the truest sense of the word. I was not yet fifteen."

"You might have been a pretty girl when I married you, but you turned into a beautiful woman when you bore my son." The woman starts to cry. Her body shakes uncontrollably.

"What's the matter, Love? Please don't cry, I didn't mean to upset you." Charles sits on the edge of the bed and holds her. Finally her shaking stops and so do the tears.

"I don't deserve you. I never have."

"What's this? How can you say that? You know I love you, and I know you love me. What else is there?"

"It's James."

"What about James?"

The woman starts to sob, "He's not your son."

Smoothing back her hair, "That's nonsense, of course he is."

"Charles, please listen to me."

The man's eyes wrinkled with worry, "Sweetheart, I love you, nothing else matters."

"I was kidnapped two months before I met you."

"I know."

"How?"

"Your mother."

"He forced himself on me. There was nothing I could do."

"Shh-shh. It's okay."

"B-bu-but he, he, he r-r-ra-ped me!"

"Sweetheart, I know. I prayed to spare you the pain."

"I have lived in fear that you might find out."

"Love, I am so, so sorry. I didn't want to remind you. All I wanted was to help you forget. Please forgive me. I never wanted you to go on suffering."

"Then you know about James?"

"What about him? We have a fine son."

"But you're not his father."

As tears sting the man's eyes, he quietly explains, "Listen here, Letty, and understand this. I am that boy's father! I may not be biologically, but I am in every other sense of the word. I couldn't love him more if I had fathered him. Think back to the day that James was born. Do you recall how happy I was? I was terrified at first, but after I heard him cry, I got down on my knees and gave thanks that the Lord had seen fit to bless us so. I was so proud; I walked around like a rooster for weeks. Oh, Letty, how could we act so foolishly? To have wasted so many years, when all I wanted was to make you happy. My Sweet Angel, can you forgive me?"

"The fault lies with me, My Darling. I should have been honest with you from the beginning."

The woman gasps for air, "*Gracias*, My Love, for being such a wonderful husband and father. Know always that I am with you."

Letty slurs, "I must rest now. My heart no longer feels heavy. I love you, Charles. I will always love you." She draws a deep and labored breath, her last. Charles leans towards his soul mate's still form and gives her one final kiss. Tears cascade over her pale face. Choking, Charles says, "Find peace My Love, for soon I will join you." He blows out the candle, leaving the embossed Madonna and child in the dark. Stooped shouldered, he walks out, leaving behind the best part of him—his heart.

Goodbye Texas, Hello Big Apple

Kimi A. Esquivel

With my boarding pass in one hand and a carry-on bag in the other, I stepped onto the plane, realizing it was too late to back out now. Butterflies filled my tummy, while comforting, reassuring comments from my friends consumed my mind. Only twenty-one years old and exercising my privileges as an adult, I purchased my own plane ticket and drove to the Houston airport without asking my mommy for permission.

Spring Break 2000: Most typical college students made their way down to the warm beaches to bask in the sun and drink until they puked. I, on the other hand, left behind little ole' Texas for the much colder temperatures of the Big Apple. Two of my best friends from high school accompanied me. Throughout the flight they assured me, as you would a small child, of my safety 35,000 feet above the ground. We landed in Memphis, Tennessee, to catch our connecting flight. On the second plane, I did not have the comfort of my friends by my side but rather two hefty businessmen who hogged the window seats.

As we flew over New York, the plane slowly descended and broke through the clouds; the spectacular sight of Manhattan's skyline came into view. I discreetly tried to see the glow of the thousands and thousands of lights from the skyscrapers. Brooklyn Bridge, a radiance of red and white lights, overflowed with traffic.

The businessmen, blocking my vision, noticed my excitement and in their thick Brooklyn accents began to point out some landmarks.

"Can you see the Statue of Liberty?" one man said pointing his chubby finger at the window?

"I don't see it," I said, sounding like an eager child.

"She's right there."

"Where?" my voice, impatient.

"Right there," he repeated.

"Where?"

During this, I could hear my friends snickering at my eager shrill, "Where? Where?" After several failed attempts to situate myself to catch a glimpse of this famous statue, she finally entered my line of sight. From where I was sitting, she looked amazing. What a sight! Standing twenty-two stories high, her torch illuminating the sky was a sight I had longed to see. As a symbol of freedom, liberty, and opportunity for many, she touched my heart.

When the plane touched down at La Guardia Airport, it was like landing on a different planet. Bug-eyed and jaws dropping, I stared at people from different nationalities who wore unusual apparel and spoke languages that sounded like jumbled up incoherence. My friends and I pushed our way through the automatic doors that led outside. The smell of gas fumes leaking from the long line of yellow NYC taxis and second-hand smoke from relieved passengers filled the air. Once our cab pulled up, a stereotypical turban-wearing driver stepped out to assist us with our luggage. "Where to?" he asked.

"Brooklyn." The driver groaned in disapproval, threw our luggage in the trunk, and made his way, with a little less caution than I liked, onto the Brooklyn-Queens Expressway.

We had made arrangements with Jobina, another old high school friend, to stay at her place. As we crammed into her century-old brownstone, I realized this was not the Four Seasons. Her living room had just enough space for a love seat and a thirteen inch television. In the back of the room, a dangerously hot pipe was enough to heat the whole apartment.

Jobina was our guide on the weekend, but weekdays we were on our own. She showed us the ropes concerning the train and bus systems (since cabs were a luxury we couldn't afford). But Monday we had no clue which trains went where, and the stations were definitely not a place we wanted to linger. Referring to maps would give away our tourist status, which we were advised could be dangerous. So most of our trip involved hours and hours of walking. Luckily we always made it to where we wanted to go.

Either brave or naïve, our little group of La Feria girls acted carefree, oblivious to the dangers of the Big Apple. We ventured to see all the sights: the Statue of Liberty, Empire State Building, World Trade Center, Time Square, Bloomingdale's, a Broadway show, *Rent*, and Central Park. We indulged in all types of foods (mostly Italian), desserts, and drinks. We gals hit all the clothing stores and shopped until we dropped. Never forgetting our loved ones back home, we bought plenty of souvenirs. I knew this was going to be a time I would not soon forget, especially since I paid for most of it with my credit cards.

Back in the Beginning
Lori Garcés

I feel my legs stiffen and my heart sink as I get out of my Ford Explorer and walk toward the old wire fence surrounding my Grandma Fela's home. I stand before this old worn-down frame home, and it's hard to imagine that at times it appeared almost regal. In my memory, Grandma Fela's house stands tall and proud on Watson Street. Her house has three small bedrooms, one family room adorned with pictures of all her grandkids on the wall, a kitchen that is open to the small space we liked to call the dining room, and one narrow bathroom with no ventilation system or window, so anyone entering it after my *Tío* Chi-Chi would take his showers would be smothered in his Old Spice after shave.

I slowly recall the days when Grandma Fela's house buzzed with life, and I can't help but smile. I loved Grandma's dining room because that's where all the fun began. There was nothing fancy about the room, a small open space with a heavy wooden table in front of the big white picture window. Grandma always had her windows open, so whenever a breeze would pass by, her beautiful white curtains would fly and get caught on one of the chairs, twining themselves like stories. Family, friends, even strangers were welcomed to sit and rest here as soon they walked in.

"Grandma, when I grow up and get married may I have this table?" I always asked hoping one day she would say yes.

"No, Lori, *dis* table it belongs to Chi-Chi or my *cuatitas* when I go to heaven *con Diosito*," she would reply with a warm smile hoping I was not offended. I never was. Grandma learned to speak English on her own because when she was young she worked for Anglo women, cleaning their homes. She would always tell us grandkids with great pride, "*Ju* kids speak to me in Englich because I know how to understand it!" And she did understand us! She understood every word which proved to sometimes be unfortunate because we couldn't say bad things about people we didn't like.

Family gatherings were always at Grandma Fela's house. The older cousins were in the back bedroom gossiping or just being too cool for everyone else. The younger cousins were either outside playing tag or sitting in the kitchen eating. My uncles sat in the living room watching T.V. Some stood outside on the front porch, to smoke and gossip in their own *machismo* way. My mother and aunts sat at the table with Grandma, catching up on the latest small-town news.

Without knowing it, they set off certain signals to us kids. We knew they were talking about someone or something really great when they whispered. We tried not to giggle too loudly when Grandma start speaking Spanish fast and angrily because we knew one of them was being chewed out. There's a certain satisfaction kids get when they hear their moms getting into trouble. We would rush up as fast as we could whenever great laughter would erupt. Sometimes they actually let us stay to listen, and then they would tell great stories about when they were kids. For example, they would laugh about the time *Tía* Mere and my mom boxed with our uncle's boxing gloves. They would describe the cotton fields they worked, how *Tía* Susie didn't have to do as much work as the rest of them because she was the youngest, or how *Tia* Tat was given so much responsibility at such a young age because she was the oldest and had such a great head for math. Sometimes my dad and uncles would come up with great Spanish jokes that made us all laugh 'til we cried. I can still picture Grandma looking like a beautiful queen as she sat at the head of the table.

As we got older, my cousins and I took our places at the table. We started telling our own school stories and laughing at our own silly jokes. Usually we just sat around poking fun at each other or any poor soul in our target range. If I close my eyes and concentrate hard enough, I can still smell the aroma of authentic, homemade, grandma-style Mexican cooking that always filled the air. Grandma Fela's singing and humming always accompanied her spices as their aromas rose to the white ceiling.

"*Alabaré, Alabaré, Alabaré, Alabaré, Alabaré, a Mi Señor,*" Grandma would chant as she rolled out flour *tortillas* and cooked fried chicken drumsticks as only she could.

All of us grandkids sat around the table, belly-laughing at our own corny jokes as we slapped sweet golden butter on the warm flour *tortillas* Grandma placed on the table for us. She would wrap them in crinkly silver foil, but with all of our chubby hands reaching in for a new one, they didn't stay wrapped for long.

"Grandma, Ricky dripped butter all over the floor because he's being a pig!" Betty would shout out. Poor Ricky. He was always getting into trouble.

"*¡Ricardo, no seas marrano! Ju* better not be being a pig, *mijo,*" Grandma would scold. We laughed as she scolded poor Ricky, but we knew better—Grandma wasn't really scolding him. She really didn't care about melted butter all over her brown 70's style vinyl floor.

Sometimes, when she would finish her cleaning and all of her yard work, she would tell us to get our change ready to play some *Chalupa. Chalupa* is a Mexican bingo-style game. She loved playing poker, but I remember Fred and Abe were really the only kids interested in playing, so she would break out the good old *Chalupa* cards in order to make all of us happy. I remember feeling true happiness as we picked out our cards and set three small bowls in the center of the table; one for *esquina*, one for bingo, and one for the *posito*. We followed Grandma's rules and didn't argue with her; she knew everything!

Up against the wall, behind the table, Grandma's brown book-shelf stood straight up like a soldier, as if it were just patiently waiting for someone to take notice of all of its own wonders. If you stood before that bookshelf long enough and quietly enough, Grandma Fela's shelves would quietly start to speak. They would whisper about the past through portraits and handmade photo collages. We could learn all about Grandpa who went to Heaven long ago. We could also see smiling faces of family members we never knew. On the top shelf sat Grandma's sacred Catholic Bible. If you looked closely enough, you could see folded down pages and note cards securing specific passages or stories that were important to her. Her black stone rosary sat neatly next to the Bible.

"Grandma, why do you pray so much?" I curiously asked one afternoon.

Grandma replied without hesitation, "Prayer gets us closer to *Diosito, mija*. No matter what *ju* can never lose *jour* faith in Him. *Diosito* will always be holding *jour* hands, even when *ju* don't think He is. That's when He is probably holding them so tight, *mija*. Promise me *ju* will always pray, Lori."

"I promise, Grandma." I simply replied without realizing how important her words would be to me years later.

When I was seventeen years old, Grandma Fela was diagnosed with stomach cancer. Her house grew quiet. The aroma of her spices and her angelic singing voice no longer rose to the ceilings. The dining table transformed from a place to play *Chalupa* to a place for crying and mourning. Her grandkids didn't laugh at jokes, and the floor remained unfortunately butter-free.

Our family, like Grandma's poor little body, grew cold the day she died. The center of our family unit was gone, and for a long time we were no longer the tight-knit group of planets that revolved around our glowing sun. Several days after the funeral, I went to Grandma's house and found myself in the deserted dining room. I stood like an angry soldier before her brown, worn-down bookshelf, feeling betrayed. She was supposed to be more than just another picture mounted in a wooden frame. She was supposed to physically be here with all of us. She was supposed to meet my husband. She was supposed to see me finish high school and graduate from college. She was supposed to hold my little Erasmo in her soft arms.

"God, why did you take her away from us?" I thought. Through my burning tears, I could see her Bible staring at me as if to whisper, "It's okay to cry, but don't blame God." Suddenly, I felt so grateful because I remembered my promise to her. I was supposed to never forget to pray. Grandma Fela helped me feel God's hands holding my own, and she wasn't even there.

I left the sad little home with my head resting on Erasmo's comforting shoulder. "She's still here, Babe. Don't feel sad, she's with your Grandpa now." His words spoke the truth, and I knew everything would be okay.

Years have passed, and once again I'm standing before the old frame home. Things have certainly changed. I notice Watson Street has been renamed Garcia Street, driving home the fact that time marches on. I no longer want to go in. I peer through the picture window which is no longer a brilliant white. Through all the dust and water stains, I can see the tainted curtains hanging sadly. I can see that old varnished table sitting lonely and cold. I can see her making her famous flour tortillas and frying her famous chicken drumsticks. Even though I'm standing outside the dining room, I can still hear all the laughter, the glorious church songs, and heartfelt prayers that once echoed in her small rooms. These are the childhood memories I have etched in my heart eternally.

Life goes on. We no longer go to Watson Street for family get-togethers. My sisters and their families, my brother and his girlfriend, and my small family get together at my parent's home on Rabb Rd. Our kids gather around their grandma's small round kitchen table laughing and dripping butter as they eat her warm flour *tortillas*. They love to be spoiled by Grandma and Grandpa, and they love listening to stories about us growing up.

One day I will be called Grandma, but that's another story.

A Mother's Love

Isela García

A gust of summer wind swirled around like a small tornado picking up dust particles and dropping them into my eyes and mouth as I leaned to look out the bedroom window. The colossal mesquite trees that stood in front of the house swung from side to side as if dancing to a soft melody, limbs gracefully moving as if teasing the sky. Yet there was something odd and dreadful about the air that made me stray from such magical beauty; even the dogs could sense it because they wouldn't stop barking. *"Parece día de muerto en Santa Rosalía,"* my mother whispered softly.

I ran toward the tallest tree in front of the house where the doves landed, surrounded me, and looked with their grief-stricken big eyes as if asking me to help them, "cuu,cuu."

"Bájate de allí muchacha, te vas a caer," my mother yelled at me from the house as she saw me struggling with a birdhouse in one hand, trying to climb the tree with the other. Even though she worked all day, she still knew where we were and what we were doing all the time. She was a seamstress, so she had positioned her sewing machine right in front of the biggest window of the bedroom. *"No me caigo,"* I responded. I was trying to put the birdhouse back since it had been knocked down the night before by the strong winds of the storm.

"Que te bajes te digo," she yelled again. I didn't listen to her and

continued climbing the tree. I felt that it was my responsibility to put the birdhouse back up so that the birds would have a place to spend the night. My bare feet kept slipping as if I were walking in mud. I wasn't even half way up the tree when my arms and legs began to get tired and my fingers started to cramp. I took one step up and slid back to the same place. Soon my feet began to feel as if they had been set on fire, and the pain of my muscles and fingers was unbearable as if someone had stuck hundreds of pins in them. So there I was, paralyzed like a lizard sun bathing. All of a sudden, I felt someone pulling the birdhouse and taking it from my hand. It was my mother. *"Te dije que te bajaras. Este árbol esta muy alto,"* she said. In fact it was a tall tree considering that I was only five-years-old and only about three-feet-tall. I descended, and as we walked back to the house, my mother told me how dangerous it was to climb tall trees. I heard her, but I was already planning ways to get out of the house to put the bird house back up on the tree without Mom noticing.

I sat next to my mother for a few hours waiting for the precise moment when she got distracted so that I could walk out unnoticed. As soon as I had a chance, I ran outside, grabbed a piece of rope that was hanging from kitchen door, and ran toward the tree. The birdhouse was still on the ground under it. I grabbed it, tied it to the rope around my waist, and started climbing the tree like a cat chased by dogs. I had to climb quickly before my mother saw me. This time it was easier because I was using both hands. As I got to the top of the tree, I found a big, strong branch that would hold the birdhouse and tied it there using the piece of rope to secure it. I checked it, and it was sturdy. My job done, I thought of how my mother had underestimated me for being a girl too small for the job. So deep into my thoughts and so enjoying my triumph, I didn't pay attention to what I was doing. All of a sudden, my foot slipped, and I grabbed for the tree trunk with all my might, but my efforts were in vain. I fell from the tree and landed hard on my left arm.

I don't remember much of what happened after that because

the pain was so excruciating it blinded and deafened me, but I do remember my mother running toward me, picking me up, pulling and straightening my arm. She knew right away it was my arm because the elbow was pointing upward. I passed out because I couldn't bear the pain. When I woke up, I was already in my uncle's truck going to town. My arm was wrapped in a white cloth with a piece of cardboard on the bottom for support. We drove for about two hours until we arrived at Miguel Aleman, Mexico—the closest town with a hospital.

I cried the whole way and my mother cried with me; she ran her finger through my hair and cleaned the tears streaming down like rivers from my eyes. "*Si tan solo me hubieras escuchado,*" she repeated softly. We arrived at the hospital and I was taken to the emergency room. I got a cast on my arm and a metal thing stuck out from my elbow. My mother said they had to use some steel pins to put my elbow back together. She told me my whole arm looked like a zigzag. It was broken in three different places and my elbow had been shattered.

I will never forget the days after that. Every time I opened my eyes, my mother was there next to me. She placed a blanket on the floor next to my bed and sat there only, leaning her head on my mattress. It was only when I slept that she slept. When I cried, she cried with me, and I was able to see that she was hurting as much as I was or perhaps even more because she felt helpless. This went on for about three weeks, until the doctor removed the steel pins.

Now when I look back and remember the agonizing look on my mother's face, I realize how much a mother can love her children. My best teacher in the school of life who taught to be kind, compassionate, generous, and selfless—*para tí mami.*

John Fitzgerald

Roel García

John Fitzgerald Kennedy lived in our living room,
Poised before the American flag:
Shoulders squared, right hand over left,
Fixed stare looking through us,
Regal and immortalized
in a velvet carpet,
Pinned on the brown paneled wall.

I was there the day my father bought it,
unpacked from a station wagon
over-stuffed with wares.
As the labor camp crowd watched,
my father tried to fast talk the Arab
who defended every buck
with wit and charm
until my father,
realized the limits of fast talking,
knew he was not going anywhere
and handed over his money
in exchange for two rolls
of carpet pieces.

Two carpet pieces,
rolled and tightly fastened,
hurled on my father's back
and solemnly unfurled
before my mother
to reveal
her living saints:
Pope John XXIII and John Fitzgerald.

For years, displayed on paneled walls
as art gallery priceless finds,
little by little, they made their way
to the place where they've remained.
Adorned with dusty silk carnations
and faded roses in grey vases,
in the company of *San Martín de Porres,*
el Santo Niño de Atocha,
la Guadalupana and la Virgen de San Juan,
protected by *el Sagrado Corazón,*
John Fitzgerald,
became part of the blessed clan
that now dwells in my mother's altar,

Not bad for someone who once lived in
our living room!

Newspaper Boy

Christina L. Garza

R unning late for church on Sunday morning, I was slowed by traffic at the intersection next to the expressway. Sitting three cars back waiting for the light to change, I spotted a young Mexican boy selling newspapers on the corner. He looked familiar to me; maybe I had seen him before, driving past hurriedly on my way to work. Now, impeded by traffic, I observed him with great fascination. He had a visible aura of happiness about him that was intoxicating, and I was entranced by what I perceived as innocence.

He was walking in my direction, paper in hand, calling out, "*¡Periódico!* Newspaper! Dollar-fifty!" The sun was glaring down on his already bronzed skin and his long dark hair was slicked back smooth from his forehead. The gel in his hair, probably *Tres Flores* because it smelled good and wasn't expensive, cast a bright sheen on hair that looked in need of a trim. His sharp brown eyes held my attention. He seemed wise beyond his age in a body too lean and small to be old. He was dressed in a pair of khaki shorts, thin from too many washings and wearings and a pressed white *camisa* with the lines visible from the many passes from his *mamá's plancha*. In the heat of the sun, with no shade to cover him, his exposed skin glistened with perspiration. Even in this light clothing, with no breeze to cool him, he looked remarkably fresh.

Behind him, next to his stack of papers, sat a gallon jug of water, half-empty in the hot noonday sun. Seemingly oblivious to the heat, he smiled and waved a paper like a great *Torero*, from car to car he carried himself *con mucho orgullo* with the paper held up in the air by slender fingers. There I sat mesmerized, as if he and I were the only people in this world, and I slowly became aware of his face as the face of my father.

By the time my father was born, his parents had survived the Great Depression and witnessed the devastation and culmination of WWII. Raising a large *familia* during this time was not an easy task on only one income. But with strong family faith and love, they persisted with grace. As *Papá* grew up, the middle child of seven, he learned the importance of family from my *abuelo* and understood the value of money when there were many mouths to feed and bodies to clothe.

He never considered himself poor. Little things like *ropa usada* passed down from his *hermanos mayores* did not really matter that much to him. He just wanted to take some of the financial burden from his young parents so he could help his family exist a little more comfortably. At nine years of age, feeling old enough to work, he took the first of many jobs as a newspaper boy. A strong-minded young man, he was determined to make a difference and to do his part for his *familia*. I wondered just how similar this boy was to my father.

Sitting in my air-conditioned car, I could not help but feel selfish while the boy stood out in the brilliant sun of the Rio Grande Valley's unrelenting summer heat. Distressed by the fact that he had to work at such a young age, I could hear my father's voice in my head saying, "*Es bueno para él. Lo hará un hombre.*"

My father, mild and reserved, only spoke when he had something to say. On the day of my *abuelo's* funeral, I heard my father say to my mother, "*Yo siempre juraba que cuando yo tuviera una familia de mí propio, que ellos no tendrían que luchar como hicimos.*" His father had given him the tools to provide for us, and he felt blessed that we were able to enjoy the *frutos de su trabajo*. By the grace of

God, we always had what we needed; we were even able to afford little luxuries, like air-conditioned vehicles, while others were not always as privileged.

"*¡Periódico!* Newspaper!"

Watching the boy enthusiastically sell his newspapers, I thought of the children selling their wares in Mexico. This boy's family probably came from Mexico, much like my *abuelos.* Living in close proximity to the U.S. border, many attempted to cross the Rio Grande in search of opportunity despite the dangers. I heard stories every day about those who tried to swim across, some with only the clothes on their backs. I heard how many were caught and returned, and about those who didn't make it across alive. It was always painful to hear the plight of my people. It was not their fault when the land was divided that they were on the side known as "*el otro lado,*" in other words, not the United States.

Despite whatever this boy or his family might have experienced or endured, it did not seem to affect him as he exuded happiness. I began to smile. What a wonderful thing for a child to be so happy! He chose to be here when maybe he would rather be just a kid. But it could be worse, right? He could be in the fields, like my father as a boy, hunkered over, yanking *cebollas* in the triple-digit heat and humidity with no break in sight. Working from sun-up to sun-down in a long-sleeved shirt and old jeans, he worked quickly, quietly, and efficiently, finding the rhythm but dreading when the field would be picked and then having to look for more work. Hands blistered raw because he could not work well with gloves. The smell of onion bled into his skin. The zest caused his eyes to sting and water, blinded by the tears of his labor. Hands that are still calloused and dirty like an old mechanics hands, dirt embedded in his nails so deeply it became a part of his skin, the earth in his pulse.

It could be worse but it is not. We all do what we have to do. *Dios sólo nos da lo que podemos manejar.* For the boy, the ink that stains his hands and clothes reminds him that he must work hard so that his family will have a better life here; seeing his hands covered in the language of this land of opportunity, he smiles. It could be worse, but it is not. He has what he needs to make it. What more could he want?

Seeing the car in front of me begin to inch forward, I realize that the light has changed. Driving up next to the boy, my window rolled down, I reach into my ashtray for my money to purchase one of his papers. I inwardly wish I had an ashtray full of money so I could buy his entire stack, then he could go home and be a child for the day. Seeing him up close, his young, confident face, I see the face of my father, and I smile.

A Rose for Mamá
Noemí Guerrero Green

It was 2:00, Friday afternoon, and Mrs. Hammonds's room was filled with fidgeting, anxious children waiting to hear who would get picked to dance.

"I know I will get picked," said Elsa smugly, "I'm the best dancer in the class."

The names of the dancers were about to be announced. These students would perform, *La Raspa*, a traditional Mexican dance, during parent's night. My palms sweated as I watched Mrs. Hammonds, our kindergarten teacher, write the names down in her notebook.

"Noemí, Bonnie, and Elsa!" she announced, "Ramiro, Mike and Jose! You six will be our dancers."

All right! I got picked! I couldn't believe I would get to dance. My *mamá* will be so proud. After the selections had been made, Mrs. Hammonds called the dancers to her desk.

"Okay, dancers, let's talk about the attire for the evening of the performance," she said. "Girls, you will need a white blouse and a red skirt. Boys, you will need a white shirt and black slacks."

Oh, no! I had been so excited about being chosen, I hadn't realized I might need a new skirt for the performance. The girls immediately began discussing where their moms would buy their outfits.

"I will tell my mom to go to Penny's to buy my skirt. You

know, they have the best clothes there," chattered Elsa.

"My mom will probably go there too," added Bonnie.

"Where will your mom get your skirt, Noemí?" they both asked.

"Oh, I don't know," I murmured. I knew perfectly well where my skirt would come from. *Mamá* sewed all of my clothes. There were eight of us at home, and my *mamá* had to save as much as possible. What would she say about the red skirt? How was I going to convince her to buy me a new skirt instead of making one? I had to come up with a plan. As I walked home from school, I decided to show my *mamá* how excited I was about the performance, so she would surely be convinced to buy me a red skirt.

Running into the kitchen, I immediately began telling my *mamá* about my day and how I had gotten selected to perform *La Raspa*.

"...and Mrs. Hammonds says I will need a white blouse and a red skirt. Elsa and Bonnie's *mamás* are getting theirs at Penny's. I thought we could go on Saturday and buy my red skirt there too," I said talking so fast I was running out of breath.

"I am proud of you for being such a good dancer *mi hijita*, and I think your teacher is very smart for picking such beautiful colors, but I think I can make you a prettier skirt than the ones they sell at the Penny's," said *Mamá* proudly.

"Oh, *Mamá!* Can't we just buy my skirt at Penny's?" I whimpered.

"Noemí, you know I make all of your clothes. Have you forgotten your five brothers and sisters? Our money has to stretch. You will see. Tomorrow I will go to Perry's and get the lace and material I need and I'll make you a skirt that will make you look like a beautiful red rose," she replied reassuringly.

"Okay, I guess," I said disappointedly.

"Don't look so sad *hijita*. You will be a *bella rosita*, a beautiful rose, in your skirt," she said soothingly.

I walked out of the room drudgingly, dragging my feet and wondering what the girls would say when they saw my homemade skirt.

The next day after school, I went home to find *Mamá* taking some bags out of the car. After she entered the house, she called me into her room.

"*Mi hijita*, come quick, *ven rapidito*, look at what I got you!" she said excitedly. I ran into the room and spied something the color of fire sticking out of a bag. Could it be? Had *Mamá* listened to my pleas and bought me the skirt at Penny's?

"Yes, *Mamá*," I answered excitedly waiting to see the skirt. My *mamá* slowly opened the bag. The color was beautiful, so I imagined the skirt. *I hope it has pleats and maybe even a small pocket on the side to carry a Kleenex or a small slip of paper*, I thought.

"Look, Noemí, at the beautiful material and lace I bought to make your skirt. The color reminds me of the rich, red clay back in my home in Mexico. It cost a little more, but if you are going to perform in front of all those people, you should look your very best. *Ven*, come over here and let's have a look.

I slowly walked over and held the material up to me so my *mamá* could see it. "It's beautiful, *Mamá*," I said dejectedly.

"Good, now run along, *mi hijita*, and let me get to work. We'll have you looking like the prettiest rose in Texas, *la rosita más bella en Tejas*," she gleefully said.

The day of the performance arrived, and my *mamá* had just completed my skirt.

"Noemí! Come try on your skirt.

As I entered the room, I could see the skirt on her bed. It had enormous petals outlined in lace like a huge red flower. I had to fight back the tears. I couldn't let my *mamá* see me cry. All I could think about was facing my friends wearing this huge red skirt and what would they say. Everyone at the performance would surely laugh and point at me. I had to think of something quick.

"Oh, *Mamá*, it's beautiful," I said trying to sound convincing, "too bad I won't be able to wear it. You see, I think I have appen— append—appendiculosis. You know the disease that makes your chest hurt. My chest really, really hurts. I can hardly breathe."

"*Mi hijita*, don't be silly, you're just nervous. I've never heard of such a disease. Hurry up now and go put on your skirt," she said laughingly.

I walked out of the room clenching my chest, trying to convince *Mamá* of my illness--to no avail. After putting on the huge rose-like skirt, I walked back into the room. When my *mamá* saw me, her face lit up and I could see sparkles in her eyes.

"¡*Mi hijita*, you are *la Rosita más bella en Tejas!*" *Mamá* exclaimed. I didn't say another word. I knew my *mamá* was proud of her work, and we were off to the performance.

When we arrived, the school cafeteria was filled with children in crisp clothes and sparkly, shiny shoes, nervously waiting to perform while their proud parents anxiously sat in their seats, hoping to get a glance of their *hijitos* and *hijitas*. Entering the cafeteria, I hid behind *Mamá*, praying that no one would see me, especially Mrs. Hammonds. If she saw me in this lacy petally skirt my *mamá* had made, she would be angry and probably say, "Noemí, all I asked for was a red skirt and white blouse, not a huge flower!"

How was I going to face her? *Maybe*, I thought, *if I ran off no one would notice. What if I tripped and broke my leg or maybe I could faint...*

"Hello, Mrs. Guerrero, how are you this evening?" interrupted Mrs. Hammonds. "And where is Noemí?"

Buenas noches, Mrs. Hammonds. Noemí is right here. Say good evening to Mrs. Hammonds," ordered my *mamá* trying to bring me forward from behind her.

"*Buenas noches*, Mrs. Hammonds," I said holding on to the back of my *mamá's* dress, timidly sticking my head out from behind her.

"Well, Noemí, let me see you. Why, isn't that a beautiful skirt you are wearing? Where did you get such an attractive skirt?" inquired Mrs. Hammonds. "I would love to have one just like it."

"My *mamá* made it," I said walking out from behind *Mamá*, twirling the skirt proudly. "She makes the most beautiful clothes. Right, *Mamá*?"

"I only make clothes for *la rosita más bella*," *Mamá* replied.

That evening I pretended I was a rose as I danced on the stage.

I had on the most beautiful skirt, and I danced for my *mamá*. As I looked out into the cafeteria, I could see my *mamá* smiling and applauding as we finished our dance. I felt like *la rosita más bella* for *Mamá.*

My Lab Coat
Mercedes M. Gurski

I couldn't stop shivering even though it was summer in Texas. This was my first day as a student observer with the Emergency Medical Technicians, and the ambulance was pulling up to the site of a three-car pile up. Tony and Mike jumped into action, dragging me behind them like a torn pant cuff.

I don't even have my EMT vest on yet, just my ratty old lab coat from school. What am I doing? I'm not ready for this. There is confusion and noise and heat and throngs of people—police, rescue workers, victims, and survivors. The site is a blur of uniforms and chaos, panic and suffering. I can't do this.

I trailed behind the guys as slowly as I could, struggling against the lead weights that seemed to have replaced my feet.

A sweating policeman ran to meet us. "There's a woman trapped in the back seat of that Ford!" he yelled.

"Is she conscious?" Tony asked as we all ran to the overturned car.

"Yeah, but she's hysterical. Won't let anyone near her."

I heard her then. *"¡Dotor! ¡Dotor! ¿Dónde está el dotor? ¡Que no me toque nadie, nomás el dotor!"* a shrill, rasping voice screamed from the tangle of steel.

I stopped right there, icy feet stuck to the blacktop and sweaty fingers choked the notebook in my hands. I didn't think a human being could sound like that.

"¡Señora! ¡Señora!" Mike yelled, fighting to be heard over her shrieking.

His boots crunched on the pieces of glass next to the shattered car window as he crouched down. She looked at him but turned her face away. He wasn't there. He wasn't a doctor. All she wanted was a doctor.

She cried louder, "¡Dotor! ¡Dios mándame un dotor!"

Mike reached for her but she pulled away, wedging herself deeper into the mangled car. Her screams cut through the air and straight through my chest. My muscles tightened and the little notebook in my hands bent in half.

Tony pulled Mike back. "We have to calm her down!"

A man caked in blood and grease broke through the police line screaming, "¡Mamá!"

Mike grabbed him and forced him away from the car. As he struggled, the man's face whipped towards me. Those wild brown eyes locked onto my well-worn lab coat, and the breath stopped in my throat.

He shouted excitedly, "¡Mamá! ¡Mamá! ¡Ya viene el doctor! "

Tony and Mike looked at each other. They were desperate. The blood drained from my head taking with it every tiny scrap of warmth left in my body.

My feet tore away from the asphalt root bed I had created. The guys pushed me to my knees next to the car and grabbed my hands. Suddenly, I cradled the fragile, damaged head in my numb, untrained hands. The woman's eyes focused on the lapel of my lab coat.

Through cracked, smiling lips she whispered, "¡Gracias a Dios! ¡Gracias Dotora!"

It was then that I understood the power doctors hold, a blind trust that allows complete strangers to save frightened lives. This power could be easily abused by lies and arrogance. Sadly, often it was. I had a lifetime of physical pain and complicated medical conditions behind me and had therefore picked up a lot of knowledge about medicine. I knew what to ask and who to trust, but the woman in the car wreck was like most of the world—she still trusted blindly the power of the white lab coat. It was for people like her that I have gone back to school. People like her that I wanted to help. People like her that I wanted to protect.

I held that woman's head perfectly still that day and watched Tony and Mike save her life. I could suddenly feel the Texas sun beating on my back, carrying my blood's warmth throughout my body. My first day had turned into my best day. I knew then that I could do this. I knew my lab coat was my destiny, my future, and my place in this world.

Boquillas
Stefanie Herweck

"I am from *Boquillas*," the man said in perfect English, pointing eastward down the canyon.

***

I had taken the narrow road perched on a canyon wall down to the hot spring. I was exhausted from long, already-hot June days in the desert; and, although even the words "hot spring" made my skin broil, I knew the spring flowed into the Rio Grande, which being neither ice cold nor crystal clear, still promised a wetness that would cool and clarify my vision.

The spring filled a pool that had been walled in with stones by early Anglo immigrants to this isolated region. Before the spacious square structure into which the spring waters now flowed, there had been a bathtub-sized hollow carved by native hands from the stone floor of the riverbank. And before the bathtub there had been only water, trapped deep below the surface millennia ago, heated by geologic forces, flowing unimpeded into the primeval ancestor of the Rio Grande.

***

"I am from *Boquillas*," the man said carefully, deliberately, and I followed his pointing finger along the wide river plain to where the canyon walls narrowed and became steeper and this present river disappeared around a bend.

***

When I arrived at the spring, I touched the water in the pool with my toe. This slight contact was enough to close a kind of circuit. Instantly, 105 degrees shot upwards through me and into the sky. I was a conduit for desert heat: the beating sun above, the scalding water below, my body the arc between them. I sloshed into the river above the spring where the lukewarm water felt like ice in comparison.

Lying down in the water with my back against the smooth stones, I waited expectantly for the glare of the heat to dissipate. But even as my skin cooled, my eyes were invaded by still more brightness. Glittering objects lined the western side of the stone wall around the spring. It was as if someone felt that the sun and the water did not create enough light. Peering out from the glare onto what lay on the wall, I could only see bright splashes of colored light.

***

"I am from *Boquillas*," the man said, and a cloud began to pass before the sun, gradually revealing details: the taut sinews on an outstretched arm, veins lining a slender hand, the slight curve of an extended finger.

***

I moved toward the objects on the wall, still apparently under the influence of the bright light trance. The source of this incredible light, bright enough to startle even in the unrelenting, unabsorbed desert sun, was a collection of gemstones gilding the top of the rough rock wall. Their variety and spacing made the ledge glow in color. There was the pure white light of clear quartz, the pink of rose quartz, the rich gold of amber, and the purple of amethyst crystals. The crystalline stones shot their beams of light into the surrounding space, creating rainbows on every possible surface while the rounded stones seemed to pulse subtly.

Here was a westward-facing shrine to the late afternoon sun, the hottest, the most remorseless god of the desert. I imagined that the construction of this altar was the final act of human beings in the canyon of the hot spring. In my mind's eye, I saw

many hands, tanned, desiccated and desperate, arranging gem-
stone offerings on the spring wall. Some of the hands had, much
earlier, decorated the layers of shale on the cliff walls above the
spring with ochre pictographs; others had formed the stuccoed
stone buildings nearby--a general store, a boarding house. But
pursued by the severe heat and unmerciful light of the
Chihuahuan sun, people abandoned the canyon and left, not a sign
of propitiation, for they had learned this god was not to be
appeased but offerings existed as a final homage to the agent of
their ruin. In the heat and light I was caught up in their reverence.

***

"I am from *Boquillas,*" the man said, and I felt the first isolated
drop, not certain at first whether it came from the sky or from the
river.

***

My movement toward the wall triggered an invisible tripwire.
Suddenly, a man came splashing across the shallow river. He
stepped onto a dry rock bar in the dead center, christening the
white, sun-bleached stones with river water, the caretaker of this
shrine, apparently, the Priest of the Sun. I stood at the shrine and
composed myself for the ceremony I was sure would follow.

But when I looked into the eager, smiling face of the figure
standing in the middle of the river, I was transported, not to
ancient temples, sacred groves, but to the *mercado.* In the turbulent
sound of the rapids I could hear the bustle of commerce, the rau-
cous hawking of vendors, the flat clink of dirty coins, *cuánto eses*
and protests. I planted my feet more firmly on the river stones to
avoid being jostled by the crowd of bargain hunters in my mind.
In one moment I was a pilgrim come to pray at a solar shrine, in
the next I was a potential customer viewing merchandise offered
by an eager salesperson. The shiny stones before me lay on the
wall, not as sacred objects surrendered to a demanding god, but as
commodities--trinkets and souvenirs offered up for my own con-
sumption. Startled by this abrupt shift in vision, by its sheer dis-
juncture, I took the evasive action of a seasoned tourist and pre-

pared my *no, gracias, no tengo dinero*. The words forming themselves in my mind felt like a fall to earth after a magical suspension
in sunshine.

My jaded negative response barely concealed my guilty knowledge of this man's desperate circumstances. As the Rio Grande,
overused and underfed, slowly dies, as the rounded river stones in
its center dry out and whiten, crossing the border becomes as easy
as stepping over a puddle. But as the physical geography of this
once mighty river has become more insignificant, its geopolitical
importance has magnified. Given the multitude of perils that
endanger our country, we are told, the border, even in this remote
desert, bounded on the southern edge by nearly impassable mountains, must be made impermeable. For tourists, crossing the border here or at the nearby villages can now result in prosecution.
This threat has dried up the trickle of tourism that was once the
mainstay of the inhabitants of the opposite bank of the river. For
this man and his neighbors, the transactions that are their life-
blood must now occur in the in-between space of the river. They
go about their business with bare wet feet, slipping on algae-cov-
ered stones. Contemplating this reality, I quailed at the man's
smile as though I were looking into a chasm. He was not a priest
come to encourage me to abandon worldly ways but a miserable
victim of the ways of the world.

But the man, my peddler priest, spoke and so rescued me from
both of my illusory visions.

"I am from Boquillas," the man said, and a cloud blotted out the
sun, and the dark form in the center of shiny rocks and sparkling
water, the devout priest reverently approaching the shrine of the
sun, the eager salesman plying his wares, the unfortunate casualty
of economic injustice and overzealous patriotism—all became a
man standing in the middle of the Rio Grande in June telling me
where his home was.

He Walks With Pride

Arcelia León

He hated riding in a car. They were a family of nine packed tightly in an old station wagon—driving all day and all night, stopping on the side of the road only long enough to eat sandwiches and take care of other necessities. He would get so car sick that his jaws would clench and his stomach would knot. Still, there was the deadline. The other workers would be arriving soon and competing for the harder but better paying jobs.

He was only fourteen years old, but my father shared the burden and responsibilities with his father of providing for the family. When they immigrated to the United States from Mexico in 1955, they did not have dreams of becoming rich. They simply wanted the opportunity to work and earn an honest living. The oldest child in a family of nine, my father did not have the luxury of choice. He was expected to work hard and help provide for the family.

The entire family would spend their summers traveling from McAllen, Texas to Wisconsin, Illinois, to Sturgeon Bay, Michigan and back again. They were migrant workers and as such had to go where they could find work. My father worked alongside his father and brothers picking everything from cotton to cherries. Their goal was to make enough money during the summer to supplement the meager earnings of the $17 a week my grandfather earned at a construction company in McAllen. Since the children were all required to attend school, summer time was the only opportunity for the family to earn enough money to survive the rest of the year.

They would rush back home to the Valley just in time for the children to start the school year. My father loved school and made straight A's. When he broke through the language barrier, he was able to advance quickly through the system. He was promoted from the fifth grade to the seventh grade, then from the eighth grade to the tenth grade. The other students hated and resented him.

They lived and attended school in *"La Zona Mexicana,"* "The Mexican Zone." Most Mexican Americans living in the Valley at the time were determined to separate themselves in every possible way from the Mexican migrant workers. From refusing to speak Spanish, and ridiculing those who did, to picking fights at school and vandalizing cars, the Valley-Mexicans did more to hurt the migrant workers than the Anglo-American did.

My grandfather had a wife and seven children, yet no one ever gave him information about government aid for needy families. He didn't know that such programs existed. The Valley-Mexicans who knew about the programs kept the information to themselves and never offered assistance in any way. There were times toward the end of the school year, as money was running out, when they didn't have enough food to eat. Not even the school told them about free lunches.

"No traía ni un centavo en el bolsillo, pero esos eran los añ os más felices en mi vida." "I didn't have a cent in my pocket, but those years were the happiest of my life," my father says when he talks about his youth.

"Dad, how can you say that? You were just a kid and yet you worked as hard as your father. You were discriminated against by your classmates and exploited by your boss. You even had to give up your dreams of going to college to help the family survive." My father simply smiles and gently shakes his head as if he holds the key to a treasure only he knows about.

"*Eso no es importante mija. Lo que sí es importante es la familia. Dios siempre nos cuidó, y yo era feliz.*" "That doesn't matter, Sweetie. What does matter is family. God always watched over us, and I was happy.

My father has a talent for finding the positive in any situation. "*Caminaba por las calles con mis amigos—pobres pero felices.*" "I would walk through the streets with my friends—poor but happy." His eyes water as he begins to reminisce. He loves to talk about his girlfriends and laughs when he tells me about not having enough money to buy two movie tickets. He would tell his date to meet him inside the theatre because he couldn't buy his ticket and hers.

After school, he would walk to construction sites and collect bottles to trade in for cash at the recycling center. A full trash bag of bottles would earn him about five cents. He would also walk through alleys behind retail stores collecting hangers that he later sold to dry-cleaners for five cents a bundle. By the end of the week he would have about fifty cents.

Longing for a cold soda one afternoon, my father walked into a soda shop where he was directed to the "whites only" sign posted up front. He looked at the sign but didn't understand. When he placed his money on the counter and said "coke-a-cola" he was thrown out on the street. He didn't protest. He didn't fight back. He didn't make plans for revenge. He didn't believe in violence. He was always taught to avoid confrontation and lead by example.

All my life, my father has taught me to find peaceable solutions. "*No te dejes llevar por tu coraje. Encuentra otros modos de solucionar tus problemas.*" "Don't get carried away by your anger. Find other ways to solve your problems."

My father refers to this time in his life as the happiest of his youth. He doesn't dwell on the negative, but rather lifts my spirits with stories of childhood pranks, sibling rivalry, and romance from his golden age of innocence. He walks with pride. He has the confidence of a man who has survived the hardest of times with perseverance and dignity.

Amá
Jozi Maldonado

*A**má*, my mom and first teacher, is short, strong, and rough. My *amá* is everyone's *Amá*, including my sisters in-law, the neighbors, and close friends. A term for many Mexican-American moms who have endured life, *Amá* is a title of endearment.

At about 5'1" now, God probably gave her a couple more inches years ago, but at seventy four, I guess you are allowed to shrink a little. Her demure size never deterred her. She is shy in a room full of strangers but not for long. My mom is like a *chile piquín, chiquita pero picosa*. She is small, but she has a bite.

Many times as children and even as adults, when we needed or wanted more of an answer, her responses were as short as she. When we would ask about our past, it became almost militarily anecdotal, "Don't ask. Don't tell." Her quirky answers often stung. People like her funny stuff; they laugh aloud. But when her comments hurt, no one says a thing. We respect *Amá*.

Wanting to do something for *Amá* always poses a challenge because she is not easy to please. We want to take her out of the kitchen, to give her a break, but that becomes a hard task to achieve. Quick to criticize her surroundings, the food, service, and so forth, *Amá* wears us down. "This room is too hot, too cold. The food has no flavor, too salty. For this kind of food, you should have let me stay at home. I could have had a *tortilla with chile, me podrían dejar en la casa.* What, there is a line at the restaurant? *No está tan bueno.* It's not that great." Often her words are chile peppers; they sting once you swallow and many times after that.

I am my *amá's* pupil. It is her drive and determination that makes me go on even when I think I cannot. When I told her that I wanted to go to college, she laughed and said, *"¿Nadie lo ha hecho, por qué crees que tú puedes?* No one (in our family) has done it. What makes you think you can?" When I graduated from college, I promised *Amá* that I would buy her a house, and we would not have to rent ever again. She said, *"Me muero antes.* I'll die before it happens." This was her same response when I told her I was buying a new car, going to be on television, buying my second house, getting married—you get the picture? I did indeed accomplish all of these things, and thankfully *Amá* is still cooking.

My *amá* has lived with me since I graduated from Texas A&I University in the summer of '91. When my husband and I began constructing our home, we took her to see the freshly poured concrete slab. She asked boldly, "Where is my room going to be?" I pointed to the general area where her room would be, and she said, *"Aviéntame con el perro, porque aquí no hay lugar.* Put me where the dog lays because there is no room for me here!" My husband and I worked long and hard on our blueprints and toiled longer on our savings to build our dream home only to have my mom crush our spirits like a *molcajete* with her mouth full of chile peppers.

Many times I have tried to grasp why *Amá* is negative, thinking that her childhood was rough. Growing up in the 1930's with only a third-grade education, many fields of dirty, white *algodón* and ripe, juicy *sandías* to reap and sow, and siblings to help raise, there just was not a whole lot to look forward to. Even with that, she managed to give birth to nine babies who have gone on to give her nineteen grandchildren and eleven great-grandchildren.

Amá is strong and as much needed as the aroma of her *ajo* and *comino,* the staples of Mexican cooking. Outliving two children, one in a tragic accident, all siblings but two, a grandchild, and many loved ones who have been buried in the last few years, she says after every funeral, "I cannot go on," but she does. Her saying lately is, "*Tengo más familia en el cielo, que aquí en este mundo.* I have more family in heaven than in this world." Physically capable of doing everything I can do and more, she moves furniture and heavy potted plants without flinching. When I ask her if she needs help, she usually tells me, "Get out of my sight! *Muévete, quítate.* I can do this." As she moves like a bulldozer, I step back, watch, and hold my back awkwardly.

She is rough. Her hands are unmanicured, and she would not have it any other way. They are big and bulky as baseball mitts from years of hard work and arthritis. You would never know that her hands ache every morning when you smell her *café* brewing, her *tortillas* blistering on the blackened *comal*, and her refried beans wafting through our rooms.

Arthritis, age, a hysterectomy, gall bladder surgery, hand surgery, and a broken wrist should have bogged her down a long time ago, but all these minor idiosyncrasies, as she calls them, have not downshifted this train. She keeps her salt and pepper hair short and over her ears, military style. Wash and wear describes the hairdo and clothes she has kept for the last two decades. *Amá* never wears makeup, unless I put it on, which she allows about twice a year, begrudgingly. As I apply a new, fresh face, she grumbles about how she is going to sweat it all off before we get wherever, and she could be mopping, feeding her birds, or tending to her plants instead of to this nonsense.

Amá is the best *Amá* and everyone's mom. She has taken care of our beautiful three-year old Hailey since her birth, and she now teaches her. *Amá* treats her grandchildren like gold. Hailey loves her *Amá*. I am blessed, fortunate, and happy to have *Amá* as my mom, dad, and teacher. I continue to learn so many great lessons from her, and I hope to be a wonderful *Amá* for the next generations to come. "*Soy hija de buena mata.* I'm a daughter of a good plant."

Family
Sylvia Alicia Mejia

The Garcia's

Talk about having a "cool" family. They sold candy, had swings in their back yard, and were religious people. Mr. Garcia had the power to heal. Once, a group of us took a duckling that was limping to the Garcia House. Mr. Garcia rubbed olive oil, said a prayer, and BOOM! the duckling's leg was better.

They had four children: Carlos and Daniel who were two or three years older than me; Toto, the baby; and Sara, the only daughter. She was a year younger than me, but that did not stop our friendship from blooming. We became great friends.

I would invite her over to my grandma's house to join me and my cousins when we played games like, *Las Escondidas, Bebe Leche, Las Cebollitas, Juduemos a Cantar, Positos, Cuatro Esquinas, Ana El Triangula del Diablo*. Once, as we were getting ready to play, I bolted like lighting over to Sara's house and pounded on the door ready to take her by the hand to share my adventures. *"¿Juanii puede salir Sara a jugar?"* I asked in the sweetest voice. Usually I had to convince Ms. Garcia to allow her little girl to play with a bunch of rough boys and girls.

Mrs. Garcia's answer was, "No." A different kind of "no," one that captured my attention. There were other no's, *"No puede, tiene que estudiar la Biblia,"* or *"No puede, nos vamos a ir dentro de un rati-*

to," or *"No puede, tiene que limpiar la casa."* I was fine with all these reasons since my mom used them as if they were written in a book, *How to Keep Your Kids Indoors for Dummies*, Chapter 1: "List of Reasons To Use When you Don't Want Your Child To Play Outside." I stood there waiting for a response, then Juanni said, *"No puede, tiene que ayudar a preparar la cena."* There was Sara, cutting a tomato with a small knife on an old woodcutting board. Sara's face was not filled with the disappointment of not going outside. She looked up and smiled, smiled? Smiled? *Why was she happy*, I wondered?

Later I got it. Sara was growing up. What I didn't get was why wasn't I doing this with my mom? I was too young to understand the high demands that come with responsibilities.

My Sister

I was turning eight when my little sister was due to arrive. I was finally going to have someone. Everyone else had sisters and brothers. It was finally my turn. "Oh my, but what about Pedro? What awful things would Pedro think of to do to my little sister?

"Abuelita" "Mami" "Pedó me quiere pegar." I close my eyes now and see Pedro's evil smirk, his eyes filled with pleasure. *Something had to be done*, I thought. As I ran to my neighbor's house, I asked myself if I would help my sister. I ran gasping for air and thinking *my sister my sister, my sister!* I stopped, grabbed an old metal toy car from the ground. I looked at Pedro's evil eyes, aimed, and threw it as hard as I could, thinking all the time of my sister. That toy car hit Pedro's head. My brain could not believe what my eyes were seeing. Tears. My eyes were wide open, my heart stopped; it took a while to sink in. Never in my eight years did I imagine that, I, Alicia the outcast, would get to see the other side of Pedro, his fat chubby butt running away from me yelling and crying for his mommy. Of course I got in trouble for hitting Pedrito, but it didn't matter. Victory was all! He cried. From that day there was no

more asking for help. There was, however, running. I ran to get away from him, and I ran to get anything in my sight to throw at him.

Corn Tortillas

At my grandmother's house, we used to sit around and thumb the kernels off the cobs. We would fill buckets with these kerns. The older people would boil them and sprinkle their magic. Then came the process that truly amazed me. They would put this mixture in a dull metal object. My grandmother would turn the knob around and around until a soft mixture would come out the opposite side. Sometimes my grandmother would let me turn the knob. Then we would make tiny balls of dough that would then be pressed flat by a different metal object. The *tortillas* would soon be ready to eat with butter and beans. After this whole process, *las mazorcas*, the cobs were left everywhere. Little did I know that the *mazorca* would help me breakthrough the fears of Pedro. The *mazorca* became my second defensive weapon against Pedro. The weapon that inspired many others weapons to come. I was a hero to myself. I had the power to go against the Great Pedro Ramírez. Soon I discovered all sorts of weapons: rocks, marbles, boards, you name it—I used it. I knew my sister would be safe. I would protect her. Like David, I defeated Goliath.

Molletes
Reyna Ortega

“Your mom said she wants cinnamon rolls. I want *cuernitos*. The ones with yellow icing,” my husband, Joe, yelled.

Joe's request did not come as a surprise. He always got the same sweet bread. Walking through *Mi Pueblo Bakery*, seeing the rows of glazed, chocolate, gooey caramel, and pecan-covered doughnuts and smelling the overwhelming aroma of freshly baked pink, yellow, white, and chocolate *mollete* made me think of *Mamá Mío*—my Grandma.

“*Es mi Mamá. No es tuya.* She is my mother not yours. No, *Tía María*, she is mine.” As a child I could not say *Mamá Mía*, so Grandma became *Mamá Mío*. I claimed her as my own. Selfishly it never occurred to me that she belonged to my *tías* and *tíos* as well.

When my cousins began to speak they too called her *Mamá Mío*. Did they know *Mamá Mío* emerged from the argument I had with my *Tía María*?

As her “Nana,” short for Reyna, I got all the royalties of a queen. She showered me with love. How special I felt on my birthday when I heard her sing:

Estas son las mañanitas que cantaba el Rey David.
Hoy por ser día de tu Santo te las cantamos a tí.
Despierta Nana, despierta. Mira que ya amaneció.
Ya los pajarillos cantar, la luna ya se metió...

Mamá Mío's voice, like that of a singing turtledove, radiated from the kitchen as she walked into the dining room with my birthday cake.

She organized a feast. We had *piñatas, tamales, chicharrones,* chocolate *caliente,* hot chocolate, and fresh baked *molletes.* I could not help *Mamá Mío* make the *mollete* for my eleventh birthday, so while I sat eating my birthday cake, I watched my brothers help her make it. Her sweet bread became famous. Everyone wanted her recipe. The aroma of heaven began to set in with the mixture of baking and the *tamales* cooking on the stovetop, plus the boiling of hot chocolate.

I anxiously waited for the clock to strike 6:00. *Los Tres Reyes Magos* arrived to deliver gifts. Since my birthday fell on the day we celebrated the Epiphany *El día de los Tres Reyes Magos,* I shared my birthday celebration with Baby Jesus. He got his gift first.

Los Reyes Magos le dieron una cobija al Santo Niño Dios para que no tenga frío durante el año, Mamá Mío announced as she opened the box wrapped in white lace revealing a radiant, almost blinding white embroidered blanket, which she took and placed over the sleeping Baby Jesus in his humble manger.

Mamá Mío smiled as she turned and looked at me. She handed me a box wrapped with a yellow bow. I opened it and found an apron. She took the purple and white gingham garment with embroidered violets and tied it around my waist. I instantly knew she had made this especially for me. How could I doubt that *Mamá Mío* loved me?

Twenty-two years have gone by.

The doors to the funeral home open wide; I take my seat in the front pew with my brothers who wiggle like worms.

On this day *Mamá Mío* is dressed in a simple black dress. Her arms are crossed; she holds a rosary and a crucifix in her hands.

Her long fragile fingers are rough with callouses from years of working in the kitchen. Like Cinderella in the fairy tale, she worked long hours displaying fortitude. *If only these fingers could move again, I think they would knead dough into perfectly round cylinders,* but alas the dough sits in a bowl waiting for her touch wondering where its maker is. She will no longer come. No baking ever took place again.

Mamá Mío's long, silky smooth, graying black hair smells of freshly baked *molletes*. From my seat, I inhale her.

I approach the casket. Now silent, those fingers feel cold to the touch, their warmth gone. As I lean over to say good-bye, I take her hands in mine, gently stroking her fingers one last time. Reaching her nails, I almost see the remnants of dough remaining as a reminder of her love. I kiss her forehead and let her go.

Joe's gentle tug on my arm brings a sea of salty tears trickling down my face. I long to curl up in *Mamá Mío's* arms and breathe her perfume, a unique blend of spices from the dough used to make *mollete*. Yet I wonder why my aunts and uncles do not continue making *mollete?* Did no one remember her recipe? Did they choose to forget it? How I wish I could resurrect her recipe to unite us once more. Instead, the day *Mamá Mío* died we lost a tradition. Yet I remain, holding onto the apron strings that once bound us together. Physically I've lost her, but my memories keep *Mamá Mío* standing firm as I continue my journey.

A Magic Moment
Jesús Pañola, Jr.

The recess bell rings at exactly 10:00 in the morning. Five hundred Mexican elementary children rush outside, excited and happy. At last some respite from this morning's arithmetic assignments! The street vendors, anxious to make money, proudly display their delicious, aromatic cuisine. Their menu includes *gorditas* filled with beans, eggs, or *chorizo*. There, look, *paletas* of many natural flavors: *limón, tamarindo, papáya, or fresa!* The children reach over the wire fence, hands eager to make a purchase. Their tiny hands like tentacles grab the morsels of food from the vendors in exchange for money. Other children in anticipation, unwrap treats prepared by their loving *mamás* and *abuelitas*.

I observe this predictable routine, this chaotic activity from an isolated spot in the playground. At times, like today, school seems to me like a concentration camp. Freedom restrained. Teachers bark orders Gestapo-like. The wire fence around the entire perimeter of the school is restrictive like a prison. But for now, I am free to roam freely on the playground. I choose to sit under a tree and watch passively. I have no money in my pockets. Envy eats at me while I wonder, ponder, and watch. And as I watch, I sense that, in turn, someone is watching me. I look around. There, in the farthest southwestern corner of the fenced playground, a boy watches me. Behind him, beyond the wire fence, stands a woman.

She wears a *rebozo* and holds something in her hands. I stare back and at once recognize the boy as Tomás, my fourth-grade classmate. That's all I know about him. Tomás begins to talk to the woman beyond the fence.

Are they talking about me? I wonder. *No, I'm paranoid,* I think. Tomás begins to wave his arms. Perhaps an invitation to approach them? I turn, look around, and decide Tomás means me. I approach them with some apprehension. *What do they want from me?* As I tentatively walk closer to them, I notice that the woman behind the fence is old. *She is older than my mother, but not as old as my grandmother,* I conclude.

She holds in her hands a container full of promise and a carafe of some type. As I get even closer, I note her weathered face, premature wrinkles, and calloused hands. I infer that this woman has had a difficult life. *The rebozo* she wears is grey, worn out. Her leather sandals have seen better days.

"*¿Tienes hambre?*" queries the woman.

I'm not quite sure what to respond. I mean, I am hungry, but my parents always admonish, "Don't talk to strangers!" Both Tomás and this woman, whom I assume is Tomás' mother, sense my reticence to answer.

Without waiting, they extend an invitation, "*Acércate y cóme con nosotros.*" Through a break in the wire fence, she hands Tomás the container full of culinary promises and homemade morsels. Tomás snaps the container open, and steam rises from it. There are perhaps one dozen tacos, lightly sprinkled with white cheese. Like a perfect host, Tomás offers the container's contents to me first. All inhibitions gone, mouth drooling, I instantly snatch a taco from his generous hands. Umm, an explosion of flavors goes off in my mouth. Don't ask me to recall exactly what the flavors were.

All I remember is that I felt an odd pleasure. "*Don't talk to strangers,*" echoed in my head, and I find myself breaking bread with them. Yet, I feel perfectly safe in the presence of these two kind, quiet, unassuming people who had somehow seen in me a loneliness, a hunger for companionship. Tomás and the old woman exchange a few quiet words. The old woman pours a hot, steamy liquid into a cup and manages to hand it to Tomás through the break in the wire fence. Tomás, in turn, delivers the cup to me. I hold the cup, sip from it, and at once discover that it is home-brewed coffee. It is coffee that, in all likelihood, had been grown, picked, roasted, and ground in the mountains of San Luis Potosí, México. Our teachers warned us that coffee was not for children, so I took a special pleasure in savoring the forbidden brew. Soon, Tomás begins sipping from his own cup of coffee. It is strange, but while we are together, sharing this magic moment, the world slows down. I mean, the crying, shouting, bickering, jeering, and cheering of the rest of the five hundred children is suddenly silenced. I feel protected from the mundane events of the world by a warm, comforting cocoon that the presence of these two kind, generous human beings have created.

Tomás offers me another taco. I look into his eyes and with an affirmative nod he releases any remaining doubts. I take another taco and mutter, *"Gracias."* Continuing to enjoy the fellowship, I take another sip from my cup, now almost empty. The old woman refills my cup, and again I glance at her calloused hands, evidence of labor and love. I mutter a sincere *"Muchas gracias,"* and take another gulp of her coffee brew.

The magic bubble bursts when the school bell rings. Tomás hands the container, now empty, back to his mother. I hand my empty cup back to her as well, and express my gratitude again by saying, *"¡Muchas gracias, Señora!"*

Tomás and his mother exchange a few quiet words. The wire fence between them prevents them from hugging each other. Tomás lowers his head, closes his eyes, and waits for *"la bendición."* At this moment, I became a spectator once again. I watch as Tomás' mother closes her eyes, mumbling words of power and reassurance. It is now that I notice the medallion of *La Virgen María* hanging from her neck. I lower my head, close my eyes, and hope that her prayers will somehow spill over onto me.

A few moments later, Tomás and I look around. The playground is almost empty, so we run to join the rest of the school children. Back to class, back to reality.

Tomás and his mother shared their fellowship with me for the rest of the school year. Every day, as sure as the sun rose, Tomás' mother fed us. That year Tomás became my best friend—my only true friend. He became like a brother to me, and his mother, a second mother. They never asked for anything in return for their kindness. To this day I love coffee, but it has never tasted as good as the first one I had with Tomás and his mother.

Two years ago I went back to visit my hometown in Cd. Valles, San Luis Potosí in Mexico. The school is still there. Its walls showed a new coat of paint. A solid brick wall has now replaced the wire fence. Memories flooded me like a torrent. I inquired about my friend Tomás, tried to find him, to no avail. I plan to go back and try to find him again. His mother, I found out on my last visit, has now passed away. From heaven, for I'm sure that's where she is, she is watching over Tomás, wherever he is. On occasion, I feel her watching over me!

Tomás

Jesús Pañola Jr

I was hungry; you fed me.
Childhood friend and companion,
I miss you so. Where are you?
Are you well? I hope and pray so.
Perhaps we'll meet again. Until then,
here is to you, a toast to childhood
friends and happy memories.

Double Trouble

Marivel Pérez

My brain seemed to drown out the monotone voice of the teacher as I stared blankly at the board and daydreamed of the approaching summer days.

"Marivel, please report to the office," the principal announced over the intercom and startled me out of my state of dreams.

"I'll be right there," I replied. I couldn't help but wonder why I was being called in.

"You have a phone call," I was told as I entered the office.

I was a senior in high school, the last of five siblings still in school. My older brother and sisters had already graduated and were doing their own thing. I always laugh out loud when I think of my mom and Marina, one of my sisters together. They are definitely two of a kind.

This particular time, I wasn't laughing. The phone call I had received in the office was to inform me that my mom and my sister had been in a car accident. I rushed home to find that they had been hit by none other than the Avon lady. Apparently she had run a stop sign, taking my mom and sister with her. Now everyone knows Avon ladies are not as fortunate as Mary Kay ladies who get to drive around in Pink Cadillacs. This seventy year-old Avon lady had a monstrous four-door, nothing-but-steel banana boat. Her steel ship had totally thrown my mom and sister into a spin, crushing their two-door fiberglass coupe. Fortunately no one had been seriously injured. In fact, the whole thing reminded me of all the past mischief the pair had been in. This wasn't the first time they had an adventurous ride, for catastrophes were a tradition for this double-trouble team. I personally think they shouldn't be let out of the house by themselves.

Why my sister even allowed my mom to drive is beyond me. You have to understand. My mom is a small person, petite and delicate. Scared of everything, you can just imagine her behind a steering wheel. The fact that they were in a car accident wasn't funny. The fact that *they* were in a car accident was. These two are like Dumb and Dumber let loose in the city.

There was the time when they took my dad's van, and my sister reversed gears into a mailbox. Then there was the time my mom scraped the entire side of the same van against a stranger's car. Poor van. Needless to say it had to be repainted.

But I will never forget "the incident." I can crack-up hysterically just thinking about it, and I wasn't even there. Again they were in a van. I will retell it as it has been told to me a zillion times.

It was a bright sunny summer day. My sister was about eight-years-old, so my mom was a lot younger and probably could drive better back then. My mom and sister decided to hop in the van and take a trip to the local convenience store we called Barbie's. I always wonder where that name came from because that wasn't really the name of the store. I don't recall ever knowing anyone named Barbie, and I'm more than positive that they didn't sell Barbies—the grill or the doll. But it was Barbie's or bust for the "Two *Amigas.*"

The family "van of the year" was a guacamole green and white replica of the Scooby Doo van. My dad designed it. He had this way of turning normal-looking vehicles into homes on wheels. No, they weren't RVs. They were just typical vans. But no van was a family van unless it had a bed, a T.V., a fan, at least three windows with tint, a C.B. radio, an eight-track player, and most importantly, an antenna so tall it would bend backwards with the wind the way a dog's ears fly back when riding in the back of a pickup truck.

Our van doesn't sound as luxurious as the modern Toyota Sienna, but this was the 1970s and 80s. All these extras were not standard features included in the purchase of a vehicle. So my dad took it upon himself to build in a bed or just weld in a bigger window.

Since we always had the coolest wheels, my sister was really excited about going to Barbie's with my mom. My parents never bought us toys at the local convenience store, but she was getting jumping jacks on this trip.

"*¡Súbete, muchacha! ¿Vas a ir, sí o no?*" my mom rushed my sister.

"*¡Ahi voy!* Marina replied as she hopped in "The Mystery Machine" and buckled up.

The trip to the store was a short one. My mom made every stop carefully, as her leg stretched to reach the pedal and her head barely popped over the steering wheel. They reached the parking lot and both got out to do their thing. While inside, Marina bought her jumping jacks and couldn't wait to get back home to play. She was ready to get back in "The Mystery Machine" and head home.

Merrily, Marina leaped into the van, this time entering through the side door. She didn't remember that she had jumped out the front door and accidentally left it slightly open. She took the front passenger's seat once again, and Shaggy and Scooby were on the road again. However, they took a different route home, neither shorter nor longer, just different.

The turn to our house was at a curve. Well, it was more like a acute angle. Every time a car turned at *La Curva*, the left side wheels would leave the ground and everyone inside would lean right until gravity pulled the car back to its normal position. In any case, an open door and a sharp curve make a deadly combination.

"Aaayy!" screamed Marina, and to my mom's dreadful surprise, the front seat was empty!

Twenty miles an hour was enough to lift the tires of this fully-loaded, "limited edition" van, and leaning right with the force of aerodynamics, Marina flew right out the front door as it swung open. Even the ten-foot antenna managed to hang on.

Brrrrrr!

"*¡Ay, muchacha!*" my mom exclaimed as she brought the van to a screeching halt. Forget what the auto world says about it taking sixty feet to come to a complete stop. This baby's wheels skidded and spit caliche out the back.

"*¡Ay, Mija! ¡Mija!*" Mom kept shouting as she frantically looked for my sister. Her biggest fear was to find Marina's body run over by an oncoming car, but my sister and her jumping jacks were nowhere to be seen. Scooby Doo, where are you?

Marina had been thrown at least twenty feet away onto a grassy area, and with minor cuts and scrapes, she once again mounted the van without having a chance to panic. She sat there, waited, and thought, "Come on Mom! Why did you have to get out?

In the meantime, Shaggy still in a frenzy, searched for her for-sure-dead-by-now daughter's body. As she looked up, she saw the van and through the van's windshield a tiny head peeking over the dashboard, static hair and all. She quickly ran to the van, relieved that Marina was alive and well.

"*¡Ay, Dios mío! ¿Mija, qué te pasó? ¿Estás bien?*"

"Yes, Mom. Can we just go home now?" my sister replied. She hadn't started crying yet, but then, like all Mexican moms do, my mom started getting mad at her as if she had thrown herself out the door on purpose.

"*¿Pues, cómo? ¿Qué hiciste? ¿Por qué te bajaste? Ay, este señor me va matar.*" The rest of the way home Mom had that look on her face. You know, that look that moms get when something terrible happens, eyes wide, as if they want to cry and yell at the same time.

When they finally made it home, Mom suddenly turned into Dr. Mom.

"*Ven, para sacudirte,*" she called.

She dusted my sister's body off with light blows to her clothes and removed the tiny stones embedded in Marina's elbow—stones like the ones you get when you fall off a bike on a dirt road. By this time my sister was shedding tears, but not because of her attempt to become a stunt girl. She was mourning the loss of her new jumping jacks.

Like in most Mexican families, my mom had a cure for everything. She was the family doctor, the clinic, the hospital, and the *curandera.* She started pulling out medicines by the prescription, not necessarily prescriptions for "falling-out-of-a-van-itis." They were more like *recetas* from some doctor in Las Flores, but to my mom they could be used for anything.

"*Tú nomás héchatela,*" she would say. "*A ver, tómate esta pastilla. A ver si te jala.*" Hey, Mom. Have you ever heard of side effects? But no one ever told my mom no. By the time you knew it, she had shoved that pill in your mouth or was already rubbing some sort of *pomada* on you, if not Vicks.

So there Mom was, treating my sister for minor injuries and *curándola de susto.* Of course, my sister was in heaven. She got to stay in bed and watch T.V. all day. Lucky her. She was careless and almost got herself killed, yet she was getting the special treatment!

Anyway, as if in an actual cartoon where none of the characters ever get hurt or die and everyone lives happily ever after, Mom and Sis later found the jumping jacks spread somewhere near the famous landing spot.

That was the beginning of a beautiful relationship. From that day forward, Shaggy and Scooby vowed always to hit non-moving objects and limit the episodes to only once a year. My senior year, they managed to meet up with the Avon lady. I don't know who's scarier.

1985
Thursday, September 17
Rodolfo Pichardo

As I slept, light began to seep through the curtains. My eyelids slowly began to turn orangy-red. I knew it was time to get up and get ready for school. After getting dressed, I walked down the stairs to the kitchen to have breakfast with my family. All the usual faces gazed at me as I entered. Vigilantly watching over the stove and drinking her coffee, my grandmother still managed to tend to all of us. Standing next to the kitchen door frame with what seemed like a dozen blueprints underneath his left arm, my uncle David gulped his usual tall glass of milk and munched on a piece of sweet bread. My Aunt Bertha, like always, danced around with a bowl full of cereal in her hands trying to get her dentist stuff together. My sister was quietly sitting and eating opposite me. And my father, he was there, too. He had just arrived two days prior from inspecting an oil-rig in the Gulf of Mexico.

After eating and after all the customary hugs and kisses and my grandmother's morning blessing, I walked to the front gate. Waving to my grandmother, I continued to walk past the front gate and ambled into the street.

Everything in the streets looked the same, but it did not feel ordinary. On my way to school I would always stop and bang on the neighbor's gate (I was too short to reach the doorbell) and wait for Juan Carlos, my best friend since third grade. I would always ask him, "What's up? Are you ready?"

He would always reply, "Yep. Do you have the soccer ball?"

Then I would always answer by nodding my head up and down while saying, "Yep!" That was our morning conversation.

So we began our mornings. Like always, we immediately started to play with the ball, pass it to each other, dribble it, juggle it with our feet, knees, and thighs not letting it hit the ground. We had not walked for long when we felt the pavement sway. Simultaneously we looked at each other and made gestures of confusion and concern, but after a couple of seconds nothing happened, so we continued playing with the soccer ball.

Then a couple of minutes later, the movement returned. This time it was more intense and rapidly became a shake. We could no longer walk straight. Everything around us stopped making sense. Everything vibrated, and even things that were not ever supposed to move were moving. The trees all around us seemed to be crying. Their leaves fell as if attacked by a chain saw. At the same time cracking, popping, screeching, and ripping noises escaped from the buildings as if they were screaming for help.

I began to sweat; my extremities shook as if a permanent chill had taken over my body. With my knees bent, my hands beside my feet, and my head lifted to the sky, I saw how the windows, unable to withstand the pressure of the contorting buildings, began to explode. Seconds later it began to rain glass: big pieces, tiny pieces, and huge dagger-like pieces!

My senses bombarded, my mind unable to process the information before me, I felt nothing. All I can remember in that instant is looking for Juan Carlos. All this time he had been pulling on the left strap of my backpack, wanting us to take cover underneath a nearby eucalyptus tree. As I stood up looking at Juan Carlos's anguished facial expression, I felt repeated vibrations on the back of my neck similar to the those of a concert speaker blaring. Juan Carlos's face changed from unbelief to total dismay. His eyes enlarged, his cheeks grew long, and with his mouth wide open, he gasped. I turned abruptly to see what it was, but before I could focus on our attacker we were swallowed by it. A dark tidal wave of gray thick dust had surrounded us in seconds. Barely being able to see and breathe, we began to feel for each other. I caught a handful of his left sleeve and held on for dear life. As I pulled him toward me, a thump hit me on the chest, instantly throwing me a couple of meters back. With my fingers firmly tangled on Juan Carlos's garment, the blow forced me to take him with me. He landed on top of me; and like a cat, he jumped up and began to run toward the light, dragging me behind him.

I yelled to him several times, "I can walk," before he slowed down enough to allow me to stand up. I hesitantly got up and began to run next to him. As we ran, without direction at first, bumping into people, cars, and other objects we could not recognize, I remember yelling, "The park! The park! Let's go to the park!" By this time the cloud of dust had lost some density, and we were able to see where we were going. We ran about another half a block where we began to feel and see grass around us. There, still shaking in the midst of the obliteration, everything was calm.

There was no noise.

No color.

Silence.

Not a single bit of sound.

The Angel of Death had come and gone.

Becoming a Bear

Abel Prado

Diego could not find adequate words in English to describe his embarrassment when a handful of hair fell out as he showered in the P.E. locker-room. He did the best he could in his alternate language, exclaiming *"¡Ay buey!"* Hair loss was a fate his grandfather couldn't escape or his father before that. But Diego's father, Roberto, was spared when he died of a heart attack at thirty-two. A thief, he breathed his last on someone else's kitchen floor during a "job." Diego was only three, but he carried faint memories of a man tickling him and kissing his cheeks—surely that must have been his father. *Padre y Eposo adorado* was inscribed on Roberto Manzana's gravestone although Diego never heard his mother say any adoring things about him. As for Diego himself— well, how can you adore someone you hardly remember?

Aside from that, the men in Diego's family were geniuses. That goes to show that life is about balance. Sure Diego was gifted intellectually, hence his I.Q. of 180, but his physical attributes were less than charming.

Growing up without a father is no easy thing. The only male figure Diego had was Gregg, a crooked cop who fed his family by shaking down illegals whom Gregg affectionately called *mojados estúpidos*. Lucky for Diego, his mom was a *mojada estúpida* with looks, so Gregg didn't mind telling his wife he was "working late."

Diego's mother, like all good mothers, tried to shield him from corruption and injustices. When she was not working one of her three jobs, she made sure that Gregg or his grandmother took good care of him. His grandfather? Well his story was similar to Dad's, except he had the luxury of croaking in his own kitchen way before Diego's time.

After Diego's ghostly recollections of *Papá*, there was *Abuela* looking after him and smiling. Right up until adolescence, Diego was under her care. It was *Abuela* who raised him. This was probably for the best, in the long run. You see the Manzana men are genetically smart, but anyone can tell you that being a helpless teen mother is no picnic. Every skill has to be nourished; *Abuela* was good at that. She took Diego to church and read him to sleep; she taught him all the basic virtues of being a good human being. Mom tried to fill in this role, but sadly morals, values, and unconditional love weren't steady sources of income, so Diego spent a lot of time at *Abuela's* house.

But one day *Abuela's* age finally caught up with her. Diego clearly remembers the peaceful look on her face that summer morning. It was a sad time for Diego. Then things got worse when Gregg's wife found out the truth about his workaholism. So now it was just Diego and his mom.

The years flew by and as Diego got smarter and his hair grew thinner, our little boy was a senior in high school. Diego had big plans, but he would soon learn that his race liked to settle for mediocrity.

The morning routines were well established. Diego would stay stuck to the sheets while Mom burned *tortillas de harina* for breakfast. By the time he got to the kitchen, overcooked ham and egg tacos awaited him. "Mom, what's that smell? Did you burn some...? Ah, the breakfast of champs."

"*Muy chistoso*, I need you to take down the stuff from the car before you leave."

"Can't Ma. Jesse should be here any minute."

"I don't know why you hang out with that *cholo*. Why couldn't you pick out better friends? You were so bright as a kid, I can't believe you hang out with gangsters now." Diego rolled his eyes, sat at the table, and forced down his crunchy breakfast. Then he muffled out, "Sorry to disappoint, Mom."

"Don't get smart with me."

"You know, Mom, God gives you relatives but good thing we can pick our friends."

"After a moment of reflection Mom snapped, "You really want me to smack you, right?" She was about to go on one of her rants, but she was interrupted by the sounds of a car horn accompanied by Jonny-O and Bonnie (the local morning show favorites of the time) playing something soothing at a thousand and one decibels on the car radio. "Mom, I think that's Jesse. Gotta go."

"Okay *mijo, que la sangre de Cristo te cubra.*" Diego never really warmed to the idea of being drenched in our Lord and Savior's blood, but it was a nice gesture, one Mom repeated often.

Jesse drove a beat-up 1963 Chevy Delta that squeaked when he hit the brakes. The interior wasn't in good shape either, but every rip and run in the upholstery made it his car.

"Hey, Jesse, what's up, man?" Diego opened the door to the car and got in. At a tone that was better suited for a stadium full of rowdy fans, Jesse, who liked to use Diego's nickname, yelled, "Hey, Calvo, a few of us are blowing off school and going to the Island. Wanna come?" Diego saw his mouth moving but he couldn't make out the words.

"What did you say?"

"I said... Wait, man, I'll turn down the radio. I said a few of us are going to the beach. It's gonna be great. We got beers and chicks and beers; it's gonna be gr..."

Diego cut him off, asking, "You're blowing off school?"

"Well you can't be in two places at once."

Diego really wanted to go but today he couldn't.

"Can't go, man. I have a meeting today with a guy from Baylor at lunch time."

"Blow it off, man. That guy will come back."

"No, he won't. He's here to see me, and if I'm not there it'll make the wrong impression."

"Why do you have to see this guy anyway?"

"Because I'm going to go to college there you idiot."

"You're going to Baylor?"

"Yeah, man. If I can get in. All I need to do is convince my mom."

"Good luck with that."

In school, Diego was average. He had a healthy amount of friends. Wasn't cool enough to start trends but was popular enough to get invited to all the parties. You know, the happy medium.

The halls of Donna High School always seemed dark and gloomy but struts down them were always his favorite thing to do. It made Diego feel important to shake hands with all his acquaintances; Jesse was his one-man entourage. It took a lot of character on Diego's part to shake hands with all of the gangsters and ignore all the macho b.s. they always gave off.

The most feared among the gangs were the Latin kings, led by Antonio Manchaca, "King Tone." Jesse and Diego hated talking to those guys but for some odd reason they got along, on a superficial level at least. At that time the Latin Kings were at war with the TCB's, so they used any excuse to fight with anyone.

"Hey, Calvo, are you sure that you don't want to go, man?"

"Nah, man I can't. Maybe next time."

"Hey, take notes for me in class."

"Like you're gonna read 'em." Jesse chuckled. Then the bell rang. The only thing gloomier than the hallways at school were the teachers. They loved to find ways to complain about their jobs. I guess some could sympathize. Who wants to work long hours for low pay, put up with terrible students, obnoxious parents who live vicariously through their children, department heads always getting after them because they forgot to fill in lesson plans, or just a simple case of the Mondays? It's tough to teach. It's sad. Along the way some of them must have forgotten why they started teaching in the first place. A few of them liked their jobs, but those teachers were hard to find. So after three and a half hours of "learning," the lunch bell rang, signaling the important event.

Diego walked over to the office for the meeting and waited. Twenty minutes later he got the go ahead.

The office was cold and shivers ran down his spine as he sat on the black vinyl chair that was colder than room temperature. The chairs were noticeably lower than the one behind the desk, so you had to look up to make eye contact with the interviewer. Diego had been in the office before, but it all seemed so unfamiliar. The pictures looked like strangers; the Michael Jordan bobble head he always loved taunted him. With every nod it seemed to look right through him as if to ask, "What are you doing here, Loser? You're not gonna get in. What? You idiot? You're wasting your time."

The spell of the evil Jordan was broken when the guy from Baylor came in and said "Hi, Kid, nice to meet you. Have a seat and let me find your file."

Travis Tuer (pronounced "tour") was a tall Anglo who nonetheless commanded a lot of respect with his perfect blend of likeability and seriousness. He looked through some files and found Diego's. Still looking at the file he said:"Well, Mister Deeago Mahnzanuh. That's you right?"

"It's Manzana, but call me 'Apple' and save yourself the heartache." The cold air made his voice crack, but it still sounded normal enough.

"Mr. Apple, Baylor is a demanding school and admission is limited. Not to mention its tough curriculum. Are you sure you have the capabilities to complete a semester?"

"Well my track record speaks for itself, and I'm not looking to complete just *one* semester."

"Okay. What do you plan to study?"

"Medicine. There aren't too many Hispanic doctors around here. Not many good ones anyway."

"Good. Baylor has an excellent medical program. One of the best. Why did you decide to apply to Baylor?"

Diego didn't know what to say, but his mouth on auto-pilot found all the words as he echoed, "Well Baylor has an excellent medical program. One of the best."

Tuer smiled. "Good one, I like your spunk... uh, how are your grades? They should be in my file." Tuer searched through his stack of papers and smiled when he found them. "This reminds me of my report card. I think that you can definitely get in. Listen, here's my card as well as the formal application."

"I have already filled out an application."

"Yes, I know, but this is for the Putnam Scholarship. A student like you should not have to worry about paying for college."

At that moment Diego felt as if his heart could generate electricity. Now all he had to do was pitch it to Mom.

For days he tried to find the right words to finesse his mom. He knew he had to do it in a public place to tone down and prevent any eruption. If Gregg ever taught him anything useful, it was that Mom found it harder to say no when she had a full stomach. So lunch it was.

The car pulled up in front of the Monte Carlo Grill at quarter 'til five on a bright day in April. The sign out front read: "Milanesa $7.99," a godsend of a price considering Diego was on a budget. He scanned the environment one more time. Satisfied, he and his mom went inside.

After the hot clarity of Highway 83, the Monte Carlo was as dark as a cave. The mirror behind the bar picked up some street glare and glimmered in the room like a crazy club scene. For a while it was all Diego could see before his eyes began to adjust. On the walls ghostly images of Mexico's famous: Pedro Infante, Maria Felix, and Mario Moreno Cantinflas stared down at customers as if it were a 1950's cantina instead of a modern-day restaurant where you couldn't smoke, let alone spit a gob of tobacco between your feet. Standing by the bar was the waiter with his tie undone and his cuffs rolled up, revealing his tattoo. The air breezed steak and fried onions. The entire scene made Diego fell a bit uneasy. He'd forgotten for a moment that he was about to upset his mom in a way that he hadn't done since Sunday School.

The waiter stepped forward and handed out a pair of menus. *"Quiren oir los especiales, hoy tenemos nuestra Milanesa a $7.99."* Diego ordered two and the waiter left.

His mom was gossiping as always, but Diego was distracted by the food. It tasted good, worth every penny of that $7.99. He didn't care for his mom's gossip, but he was listening, listening carefully, just waiting to tell her about his meeting with Tuer.

"Did you hear that Aracely got pregnant?"

"She did? Who is the father?"

"Dunno, I don't think she does either. Oh, and your *Tía* Miranda is coming down from San Antonio, so I want you to cut the grass and cleanup around the house. You know the way she is."

"Ok, Mom."

After a little bit of small talk, Mom finally left an opening. "So how was school?"

"Great. I met a man from Baylor. Where I am applying. It's a good college.

With her mouth half full, she cut him off, "Baylor? I thought you were going to Pan Am? We agreed that you were going to stay close by and save some money. Isn't that what we said?"

The mood completely changed, Diego began to regret taking his mom to such a public place. Timidly, he tried to answer. "Yeah but..."

"But nothing. You're not going to move away."

"Mom, Baylor is not that far away."

"Where is it?"

"Waco." It might as well have been on an island 10,000 miles off the coast.

Nearly choking on her food, she jeered loud enough to make everyone in the room turn their heads. "Waco!" And here it came. *"Tas loco.* There is no way that I'm letting you move away to Waco."

"I'm not moving away, I'm just going to... uh... visit... for about four years." Diego said in a calm voice, attempting to tone down the scene.

"And what are you going to study?"

"Medicine. They have a great progra..."

With a unsubtle mixer of anger and ghettoness she yelled; "Medicine? *Que chingados sabes de medicina.*"

"Mom, I know a lot about medic..."

"Shut up, I'm talking."

The sound of his mother's voice got under his skin in a way that only a mother's could. She added salt to this wound by adding one of her favorite phrases, *"Ni te puedes limpiar la cola y ya andas ahi de fantasioso."* Mockingly, she followed this up by saying; *"Quiero ser doctor. Muy chingon."*

"I can wipe my rear, Mom."

"Don't mouth off to me"

"Mom, You're always doing this. You can't keep me here forever."

"How are you going to pay for this?"

"I can get a job."

Then came a line Diego hadn't heard before, "Well, you got it all figured out don't you? Listen, life isn't fair. It's cash and carry. Sometimes you pay a little, mostly you pay a lot. And you know your father didn't leave us off that well."

"Why do you always talk about Dad like he ran off instead of died?"

"Because he might as well have run off. All he left us was a huge stack of unpaid bills, a debt to all of his gambling buddies, and a crappy apartment full of roaches."

Luckily the waiter came with the bill and closed his mother's mouth that had become a Pandora's Box.

The ride home was quiet—perfect condition for Diego to examine what had happened in the Monte Carlo Grill.

Guess his theory about a full stomach was wrong.

With the house simmering with tension from the *Milanesa* drama, the phone rang. It was Jesse. "Mom, there's a party at Eddie's. Can I go?"

"No."

"Please. I'll rub your feet when I get home."

"I said no!"

"Come on, I'll put cream and everything"

"Fine. Be home before twelve. *Que la sange de Cristo te cubra.*"

"All right, Mom."

Jesse was giddy with excitement on the way to the party. "Hey, Calvo, we have to pick up Kassie on the way there."

"Ok."

Kassie was the girl so appealing for the strangest reasons. Most guys liked her because she was interesting in a simple kind of way. The girls liked her because she wasn't really a threat, just a straight shooter with a nice smile and a neat little bow on top of a nice package.

Kassie came out of her house and got in the car. "Hey, guys."

Both Jesse and Deigo answered back in unison: "Hey."

"Hey guys, have you seen that *Dangerous Minds* movie?"

"No, I haven't."

"What about you, Jesse?"

"No."

"You guys should watch it; it's really good."

Diego got a scrunched look on his brow, the kind that appears when you're on to something. "When did you see it?" he asked.

"Last weekend with Abel."

"What do you mean, like a date?"

"Well he did buy me popcorn, so I guess you could call it one."

Eddie lived next to a big field off Sites Road, a street that was all over the news at the time because the mutilated body of a boy named David Cardenas had been dumped there. Rumors were it was gang related.

The party was pretty fun. But then King Tone showed up with his gang and a universal "aw, no" feeling filled the air. Everyone could sense it. Just by the look in his eye you could tell King Tone was edgy. All he needed was an excuse.

About five minutes later Tone shouted: "Hey, man, you looking at my girl?" There it was. The poor sap who was about to get his rear kicked answered, "Nah, man, I was just looking for something to drink." His voice trembled with every breath.

It didn't take long for a fight to erupt. No one was sure how many people got involved, but Jesse got lost in the confusion. When the dust cleared there was only a kid lying on the ground, moaning in pain, and holding his side. It was Jesse. He was the poor sap. Now they knew why they were never supposed to disrespect the friendship: Lesson learned.

The place turned into an anthill with all of the worker ants rushing into the hole when it rains. Diego was running against the traffic, bumping into faceless people as he made his way to Jesse. "Oh, no! Jesse, don't move. Just stay still. Somebody call an ambulance." There was blood everywhere. "You're bleeding a lot, man." Diego took off his shirt while he examined the wound. "It's all right, man. I think it hit your lungs but your heart rate is steady. Keep breathing, man, just keep breathing. If you don't your lungs will fill with blood."

"Calvo, d–don't let me die here, man." The terrified tone in Jesse's voice was a sound that would keep Diego up for nights to come.

"Shut up, man. You're not going to die. Somebody get a freaking ambulance." Diego used his shirt to apply pressure to the wound. He managed to stop the bleeding but by then Jesse had passed out. Finally the ambulance got there.

The next morning Jesse woke to beeping machines with Diego by his side. "Calvo, what happened, man?"

"You got in a fight."

"Did I win?"

"Yeah, man, you clobbered him."

There was a knock on the door and Diego's mom walked in.

"Diego, *mijo*, are you okay?"

"Yeah, I'm great, but Jesse's got a headache."

"There you go again with the jokes. You're going the right way for a slap."

"Whatever, Mom."

"Jesse, I talked to your parents. They are on their way. You're lucky to be alive, son. The doctor said that if the bleeding hadn't been stopped you could have bled to death."

"Calvo stopped the bleeding. I remember that before I passed out."

Mom turned to Diego and smiled, "Well, how does it feel to be a hero?"

"This is what I want to do for a living, Mom. I can be good at this, really good. But you just have to let me. Just let me grow up; I'll still be your little boy."

"This isn't this Baylor nonsense again is it? We already talked about this."

"Look, Mom, I saved Jesse's life tonight. And I can do it again for someone else. Please don't rob me of this."

"You can learn about medicine at Pan Am."

"Mom, Pan Am doesn't even compare to Baylor."

"Well make the best out of it; be here with your mom."

"Listen, it's not like I'm just going to leave for months at a time. I can come down on weekends and holidays. I'm not just going to leave. You're my mom, no one can replace you."

"You're serious about this aren't you?"

"I got a card from one of the representatives." He took it out.

"Well how are you going to pay for this?"

"The guy on the card is supposed to help me with that."

"My god, I'm getting old." Then Diego and his mom shared an affectionate hug and she said, "Well go give him a call."

"Okay, Mom. Thanks for this. I'm gonna make you proud, you'll see."

"Jesse, still out of it?" she asked, "Are you going to leave me too?"

Mom's light laughter followed Diego as he rushed to the phone. "Hello, Mr. Tuer? Yes, sorry to call so early but can we talk about that Putnam Scholarship a bit more?"

Las Gallinas

Inocente Ramírez II

When I was young, hardships met life's handouts. Little schooling, little food, few friends, and hardly any security—that was my life until *las gallinas* came. They and my mother helped me realize the intricate machinations of the adult mind, crossing me over from childhood to young adulthood.

We had just moved into our new home. This happens quite often to a young migrant boy. Luckily my mother had found us a house in rural South Texas, our home base. Mother set to work making the house habitable. That's when she noticed *las gallinas*. She became a woman possessed because she wanted one of those chickens for Sunday dinner.

Mother, a woman who bore ten children, awoke before the sun. The rooster and his harem of hens had awakened her. *¡Ojalá, que hoy pueda conseguirme una gallina!*—I hope I'll be able to get me a chicken! she thought. A woman of many scars left by life's situations, her red beauty mole near her left eye defied life's tribulations.

"*¡Levántate!* Wake up! It's time to go to school! I'm not telling you again!" She always insisted we attend school no matter what.

"You have to keep up with those *güeros*, you know!" she would intone every morning.

Being an ever-resourceful person, she packed our school lunches since the cafeteria lunch was too expensive. Sometimes one of my brothers, usually Oscar, came home after school complaining of the absence of bologna between the bread slices.

"I told you to get ready!" "No, I don't know where your socks are. I think they're still in the box." Her method of preparing the lunches was like a Ford Motor Company assembly line. It included ten slices of bread in a row with the necessary condiments at the top center part of the wobbly kitchen table. Down the row she'd move: bread, bologna, condiment, bread.

We lived in desolation, surrounded by ancient weathered mesquite trees, prickly cacti, and lots of rattlesnakes. This place resembled the last remnants of a ghost town on a Western movie set. A winding, dusty *caliche* road took us to our salvation--school. We had to trek all 5,280 feet to get to the bus stile. Mother would follow part of the way and then stop, planting her feet firmly like fence posts. She patted her disheveled hair back in place and returned to her house. A sideways glance alerted her to the presence of *las gallinas*. The chickens must have taunted her because they were aloof in their business of pecking and clawing the earth. She picked up a *leño* and threw it at them. They scattered, jumping and squawking, leaving a trail of downy feathers on their way to their roost, the mesquite tree behind the house. *How wonderful it would be to make fried chicken for supper!* she thought.

A man, the previous tenant, interrupted her wishful thinking one morning. Alarmed, she grabbed her *palote.*

"*Señora Ramirez, vine por mis gallinas*".

"*No hay gallinas.*"

The man scurried behind the house with Mother, *palote* in hand, following him closely. He surveyed the surroundings but found nothing. Providential, it seems, in trying to catch them earlier, Mother had shooed the chickens far from the house. He boarded his dirty pick-up and after a few false starts left in a trail of dust.

Times must have gotten worse because upon our return from school, we watched her rapidly pacing. The bare cupboards forced her to formulate a plan of action in getting her chicken. She convinced me to climb the tree to get her one.

"Hazme caso--tienes que esperar antes que salga el sol." This order preceded a yank to my ear because I always daydreamed, so I always seemed to receive her wrath.

Early the next morning, I began my ascent up the tree. Slowly, carefully, grabbing hold of the rough bark with bare feet, I inched my way toward the chickens. They roosted docilely on the highest branches of the mesquite. I paused only to take out a thorn deeply embedded in my hand. Not wanting to alert the chickens I became catlike. I silently progressed to the desired spot. Sweat trickled down my forehead plastering my hair to my head. *I'll be in mother's good graces if I can get her a chicken,* I thought. I looked up at the sleeping chickens, my mind sorting out options in order to grab one.

I inched closer and reached for my prize when a noise from the house startled *las gallinas.* They squawked and flew haphazardly into each other causing much havoc. Blindly I grasped for them, and to my amazement I caught two. The flapping wings, the pecking beaks, and the clawing talons bruised and bloodied me, but I caught two *gallinas!* I smiled triumphantly because this guaranteed me an entrance to my mother's good graces forever.

"¡Amá, aquí tiene sus gallinas!" I shouted happily to the sleeping household.

Mother immediately wrung each chicken's neck. They bounced back and forth, stumbling, bumping into our feet in a wild dance. She shouted for boiled water in the washtub, and her prized possession, the kitchen knife. Her face displayed anticipatory abandonment during the butchering of the chickens. She gutted each with gusto. The bloodied heads, the scaly legs, and slimy entrails landed in the trash heap where the family dogs argued over the choice pieces. While the chickens soaked, she gathered us around her and explained the process of depluming. Our constant chatter sounded like chickens as we plucked the feathers. When we finished, the backyard looked like it had snowed.

As Mother prepared the chicken, we played. The front porch served as our theater in-the-round, and oftentimes we would re-enact movies we had watched on the broken-down RCA television set, now a family heirloom.

"*¡Ya están las gallinas!* We needed no second invitation.

The aroma wafting from her kitchen had our mouths watering. We went to the communal *lavamanos* and washed our hands. Before the meal, we prayed, and then everybody got busy eating those chickens!

Afterwards Mother ordered us out of the house so that she and the older girls could clean up, so we continued our re-enactment of "Captain Hood and the Damsel in Distress." Spiraling dust above the caliche road warned us of an approaching visitor. The littlest one ran to tell Mother. We surrounded the dusty pickup truck immediately and stood on our tiptoes to look inside. The man quickly got out of the truck.

Mother frantically ordered the girls to clear any evidence of chickens from the kitchen. She covered what little chicken was left with a tablecloth.

"*¡Ahora qué quiere ese viejo!*" As she opened the torn screen door and stepped onto the porch, she busily dried her hands on her apron.

"*Señora Ramírez, vine por mis gallinas.*"

"*No hay gallinas*—There are no chickens." I stood nearby watching the world of adults. *What is going to happen?* I thought.

Pulling on his tooth, Oscar said, "*Nnguh...there are no gallinas here!*" While saying it, he picked at the chicken meat stuck between his teeth. The man merely nodded until something caught his attention. Something had landed at his feet.

A sudden gust of wind, as if pre-ordained by destiny, had propelled the chicken feathers from their resting place in the back. Mother continued her denial of *las gallinas* when one, two, three feathers, followed by a myriad of more feathers, settled at our feet. My mother could no longer deny the chickens, so she simply stated that she had to feed her children.

As I reflect on this incident in my life, I fondly smile. It reminds me of the Mexican dicho: "*Cada que miro mis jacales me acuerdo de mis gallinas.*"

Forty-Eight Hour Birthday

Andrea Rivas

"*Te dí el nombre de San Andrés,*" she'd say with conviction. "*Naciste el día 30 de Noviembre que es el día de San Andrés.*" Many families hold to the Mexican tradition of naming babies after the saint of their birth date noted on the Catholic calendar.

Most people don't remember when they learned their date of birth, but I certainly won't forget when I learned mine. The teacher's name, face, and the grade I was in have all but faded from my memory, but the incident still lives vividly in my mind. That morning, the teacher wanted to know if we knew our birth date, so she asked each of us to stand, state our names, and tell our date of birth. Sitting there waiting my turn, I felt confident. I knew exactly when I was born. In all my short six years of life, my mother had never missed a birthday celebration.

I jumped up as my name was called, filled with self-assurance, and blurted, "November 30, 1950." I'll never forget those cold eyes as her smile slowly disappeared. She glared, not at me, but at the paper in her pale, wrinkled, blue-veined hands.

"Wrong, young lady. Go home tonight and ask your mother when you were born. You certainly weren't born on November 30, you are wrong, wrong, wrong. So, check with your mother tonight and bring in the right date tomorrow!"

A century seemed to pass before all her words filtered through my mind. *How could I be wrong?* I thought as I slid into my seat, laid my head on my hands, and stifled my cries inside. My mother's words echoed in my brain, so I knew that I was right. I'd prove the teacher wrong tomorrow.

That afternoon I made record time running the two blocks to my house. I hurriedly surveyed the small kitchen then ran into the center room which served as both living room and bedroom. Mother sat at her antique sewing machine and scarcely looked up as I stomped in.

"*Bueno ¿y qué prisa traes?*" she asked, as I searched my mind for words.

"Isn't my birthday November 30?" I blurted out. "The teacher says it's not!"

She looked at me in bewilderment and said, "*Bien, bien, vamos a ver. Aquí tengo todos los papeles.*"

She pushed the cloth of a flour sack that would soon be my new dress, or my brother's shirt, or a pillow case, or part of a quilt, into the machine. Then with determination, she walked over to a portable closet. With her third-grade education, my mother kept all her files intact. Her filing system was not a fancy filing cabinet or a strong safe but the little mirrored cubby of the portable closet. She reached up and from the top of the closet pulled down a thick, yellowed string with an attached key. She opened this secret, enticing file, vigilantly removed a cigar box, and flipped the lid open. She found my birth certificate carefully tucked away behind the car insurance and the mortgage papers.

"*Aquí está vamos a ver,*" she said as she gently unfolded the crisp document. She read slowly the English document and then stopped at the time and date of birth.

"*Estos viejos mensos,*" she declared. "*Mira lo que hicieron.*" My sweet mother, whom I love very much, never really touched us in kindness or in anger, so I can't say she put me on her lap and told me a dramatic story in kind and soft words. Instead, she angrily directed a story of misunderstanding to a daughter who was already hurt by being wrong. She told me that on the date of my birth my dad had been drinking as he often did. He wouldn't hear of taking her to the doctor until she was absolutely sure it was time *"¡para parir!"* It turned out my dad was right. Why interrupt a drinking binge when ten hours of labor still lay ahead.

In 1950, deliveries were done at the doctor's office unless a complication arose. The doctor lived next door to his office so there was no need to call ahead. Late that night they drove to the doctor's office which was right outside of town. My mother says she delivered at around 11:30 p.m., November 30. She had been studying the Catholic calendar for several days, so she knew the name I'd carry and told the doctor to name me after St. Andrew. He and my dad decided to first celebrate the birth by opening a bottle of liquor. By the time the celebration was over and the paper work was to be signed, it was 12:45 a.m., December 1, and he wrote that as my birthdate. My mother hadn't noticed the error until that very moment. Now my predicament left me both right and wrong. My mother became angry, remembering this as just another thing my dad had messed up.

From that day on, I've had a forty-eight hour birth date. My mom celebrates my birthday every year with all the flair and frills on November 30, whereas my dad, who insists that he was right, celebrates it on December 1. I've never thought of changing it because I love them both dearly, and I cannot pick sides.

For years and years my mother would call and say, *"Ven para celebrar tu cumpleaños, mija."* I'd arrive to find my brothers present, waiting to enjoy chicken *mole*, rice, beans, potato salad, carrot salad, and a huge cake.

Then as we were all getting ready to depart, my dad would announce, *"Qué bueno que vinieron todos, hoy. Mañana vienen para celebrar el compleaños de Andrea."* My brothers would groan but show up the next night for barbecued chicken, which was just as good as *mole*. Even though my mom still had to cook the rice, beans, potato salad, and carrot salad, again, she always had her say.

During the past ten years, I've gotten calls to wish me happy birthday. Mom calls on November 30; Dad calls on December 1.

My mom is eighty-two now, and my dad is eighty-eight. This past year was the first time I didn't get those birthday calls—not because they've passed away but because their memory has grown frail and weak. I went to see them—on both days—scared they'd say, *"Y esta ¿quién es?"*

My Friend Neto
Francisco Rodríguez

Every child should have some magical days when they are growing up. I remember some of mine.

In the *barrio*, a group of boys always hung around together. There was me, Francisco; I was called *Pancho*, the talker because I hardly ever shut up, and I also took many dares and unnecessary chances.

My older brother was Juan, he was the *gordo* or fat one of the group. There is always a *gordo* in every group of boys.

Another set of brothers was Nune and Juan Chema. *Nune* means Junior in Spanish. I never knew Nune's real or first name; we just called him Nune.

Juan Chema was the younger of the two. I think everyone just called him Juan Chema so that we could tell him apart from my brother Juan. I don't know the source of Chema. I don't think anyone of us guys ever knew. Sometimes we called both of them Los Chemas.

There were also three other brothers that hung out with us. Fernando was the oldest we called him Nando. He was the loudest and smartest of the three. Arnoldo was called Black Sambo because he was dark skinned. (I guess kids can be mean at times.) The youngest one of the three brothers was Oscar, the *Güero*, The Light Skinned One. He was also the youngest of the group.

Then there was Ernesto or Neto!

Neto and his family were what you would call today "recent immigrants." They were from Mexico. We didn't know much about his family because they pretty much stayed to themselves. I remember that he was skinny. I mean extremely skinny! I was skin and bones, but Neto was skin and veins! All the families in the *barrio* were poor, but Neto's family was poor with capital letters! During the Christmas holidays, his family never even had a Christmas tree. I don't think they ever celebrated Christmas at all. He also hardly ever sported new clothes, or shoes, or toys. We didn't care; we saw beyond that, because we were *camaradas*, friends!

Neto seemed to have special powers like the ones super heroes have. He was smart, could run as fast as a bicycle, and could even jump off tall buildings. Neto was an unusual kid all right. He took school books home and brought them back to school the very next day. You think that was weird? He even did his homework every night!

"Netooooo, *vamos a jugarrrrr*, Netooooo, let's go playyyyy," we would yell to him from the alley next to his house.

Neto would come and talk to us through the old torn screen on the window, "No *puedo*, I am doing homework."

My brother and I shared a bicycle that we both rode to school every day. During lunchtime my brother took me home on the bike as fast as he could so that we could be back to school on time. Some of the other guys paid the twenty-five cents to eat in the cafeteria. Fernando and other students were allowed to work in the cafeteria so that they could eat there for free. Neto ran all the way to his house, ate, and then ran all the way back to school with plenty of time to spare before the next class period.

I remember occasions when my brother and I rode the bicycle really fast to get home for lunch, and Neto would run along side our bike. He kept up all the way without breaking stride. We arrived home, which was about one mile away from the school, and Neto continued running for about two more blocks to get to his house.

As soon as we sat down to eat the delicious homemade *tortillas,* the beans made in the *olla de barro,* and the *arroz con pollo* with just the right amount of spices in it that our mother had prepared for us, Neto was back for us on the run to go back to school.

Mom amazed by Neto's fast return asked him, "*Neto, ya comites,* you ate already?"

"*Sí,*" Neto answered.

"*Pues, ¿qué comites,* what did you eat?" Mother continued the interrogation.

"*Un huevito,* one small egg," Neto would say bashfully, shaping his hand to look like a half bloomed rose, to show the size of a small egg. Mom would offer him something to eat but Neto always refused.

We went through this same routine many times, but I don't think Neto ever ate anything other than *un huevito.* Maybe that was the secret to his super powers.

Our long summer days were used up by playing *trompos* or tops, making kites and trying to fly them, and marbles. The game of marbles took skill and strategy. If you were going to win, skill and strategy were important because we almost always played for "keepies." That meant that if you lost, you had to give your marble to the kid who beat you, so we didn't ever want to lose. And it was not much fun playing for "fakies," which meant that the other guy did not get to keep your marble if you lost.

Most of us shot the marbles basically the same way, curling the fingers inward toward the palm of the hand. The forefinger was used to point the marble in the direction of the intended target, and the thumb was used to thrust the marble forward over the barren ground that looked like an abandoned miniature football field with the marbles as the football players.

Neto was a skillful player, but he did not shoot the marbles like the rest of us. His unique method was to pinch the marble between his thumb and his index finger. He squeezed hard enough to project the marble forward quickly and accurately, hitting his opponents' marbles more times than not. We tried to teach Neto the right way to shoot marbles, but we were not successful. His method worked just fine for him, winning many marbles from the rest of us.

When we got bored of the *trompo* playing, kite flying, and the losing and winning of the marbles, we looked for other more adventurous and daring feats to conquer. We climbed our houses and dared each other to jump off. The houses weren't too high, but you could get hurt if you didn't know how to land. On one jump, I hit my mouth with my knee, and my teeth cut into my lower lip. My friends kept telling me, "*Te cortates*, you are bleeding." That stopped me from jumping off rooftops for a while. All of us could jump off our houses, but that seemed to motivate Neto to try something different.

He climbed a house, ran fast across the roof, and flew over the ground below toward a giant mesquite tree close to the house. It was spectacular! He seemed to fly forever through the air in slow motion. He looked like Superman for a while and then slowly the image transformed into Tarzan grabbing a tree branch and swinging down softly onto the ground. We were stunned! No one ever repeated that same feat. I believe not even Neto tried it again.

I remember my father telling me many times, "*¡Tus verdaderos amigos, los podrás contar con tus manos y no más!*" What he meant was that there may be many acquaintances but there is only a handful of true friends. I can truly say that Neto was one of those few true friends during my childhood days. He was part of those childhood magical days of my life that were then and are not now, days that will remain forever within me and within those who were there to experience the magic.

A little over forty years after those magical childhood days, I ran into Neto and his twenty-year-old son. I told his son, "Boy do I have stories about your dad's days in the *barrio*. We need to get together someday to talk about those days."

Neto just smiled. He still looked like a quiet, mild-mannered Clark Kent, but I know the real Neto!

A Cry for Help
Magdalena Salinas

I loved to play at the old branchy tree that stood in front of Grannie's yard. An aged, but strong branch as big as a log held an old rusty swing. One could hear the branch squeak almost as if howling for help when children swung back and forth. The swing was not only a toy to play with, also it symbolized the memories of generations who amused themselves with it. If the old branch could talk, it would have many stories to share, mine in particular.

About six o'clock in the evening my mother was fixing dinner, and I was outside playing. I enjoyed the pleasure of having the swing all to myself without having the bother of taking turns with my brothers and my cousins.

Before my mother went inside, she said *"Magdita, te voy ha estar viendo desde la ventana de la cocina, nadamás no le vayas a dar muy recio porque te puedes caer y lastimar. "¿Está bien?"*

"Sí, Mamá." I smiled.

Time passed and I tired of being alone. I knew *Mamá* was in the kitchen because of the aroma of food that filled the air with spices that tickled my nose. I could hear the pans as she moved them from place to place as if playing some kind of melody. I could picture her mixing and turning whatever she was cooking or baking.

I gathered speed as Mom formed flour *tortillas* and made sure the others wouldn't burn while cooking. *Adventure!* I thought in excitement. Without much more thought, I pumped with more strength. My legs stretched to grasp as much flow as possible in order to swing higher in the air. *How nice it would be to fly just as a bird does*, I imagined.

"*¡Te estoy viendo!*" mother yelled.

I knew she wasn't. She was too busy cooking, preparing for dinner. I took advantage of the situation. I kept gaining more and more speed. Once I swung up so high I seemed to be the sky. I felt as if I were flowing in the air. Without thinking, I let go of the ropes to feel the breeze all over my arms. My hair blew every which way. My cheeks filled with air as I stared with awe up at the clouds. They looked like cotton candy. Extremely fluffy, I could almost taste them.

Suddenly I felt as if someone were pulling me forward. I realized I was not holding onto the ropes of the swing. No one was pulling me anywhere. The air pushed me from behind. When the swing went up, it came back down. That was just what happened. *A little too late for salvation!* I thought with fear. Frightened and desperate, I tried to grab onto the ropes. But there was no escape.

"Mom!" I screamed, terrified. "Mom!" It seemed as if the air had scattered and blown away the words of panic. In an instant everything went black. Silence took over.

After what seemed an eternity, I felt someone dragging me to a bright light. At the end of light, I saw a shadow or two or maybe three. Then the blur of a person talking to me or so I thought. Far away I could hear my mother crying. "*Por estar al pendiente de la maldita comida descuidé a la niña. No debí dejarla jugar sola. Perdóname dios mío.*"

"*Todo va estar bien,*" my father said calmly, "*dice el doctor que solo fue un raspón.*" "*Pronto se le cicatrizará. Ya verás y al rato va andar jugando de nuevo.*"

Just a scratch! I thought in disbelief. If only he could feel my intense pain. A sharp pain ran through my head to my chin, around my neck, down my spine, and back up again to my chin.

I burst out in a loud cry as if I had awakened from a bad dream only to find out it was real. Everything from the swing, to the fall, to the doctor's office was true.

When my mother unblurred in front of me, I cried louder than before. I felt my lungs explode in a rage, pushing out of the cave that enclosed them. *Mamá* took me close to her, making sure not to hurt my injuries. Her hands trembled as she rubbed my back in comfort. Nothing compares to the feeling of warmth from the person who loves you the most. *Mamá*'s hugs and kisses were the medicine I needed.

"*Ya no llores, todo estará bien hijita,*" she said in a loving, but scared voice. Even though she was there, I didn't stop crying for a long time. I knew I was safe, as safe as a four-year-old can be.

I still have the scar under my chin. Whenever I look in the mirror, I see that swing.

The Embedded Truth

Marisela Salinas

An old black wallet rests on my mother's desk, wrinkled at the seams, still giving off a rich leathery smell. I carefully open it, anticipating, knowing its owner. My grandfather carried that wallet. The license inside reads, "Gregorio Salinas, height—5'11", eyes—brown, expires—6-21-1977." Taken aback, I take a deep breath, sigh, and began to reminisce.

My grandfather, Mr. Gregorio Salinas, was a great man. He left an impression on me and did this within a short time since he passed away when I was only four years old. What an unthinkable pair we were, a four-year-old girl and a seventy-six-year old man. Yet our relationship was as if we shared one soul, and it dwelled in each of our bodies. Never did I want to be separated from this old man. He exuded so much strength, bravery, and respect. I felt safe at the sight of him. He was quiet, though his eyes spoke many words. Pain, wisdom, and love, gained through trials, tribulations and milestones in meeting God's fortune aged his face.

Through time I heard many stories of his life and came to realize the source of all his knowledge and pain. One story goes like this: On a dark clouded day, nearing sunset, Gregorio was tending cattle when the hairs on his arms rose as a cool breeze blew in. The cattle became agitated when unexpectedly two of his uncles rode in on horseback with fear in their eyes and the blood drained from their faces. "They're after your father," they said. Gregorio instantly mounted his horse, and they hastened off in search of the hunted.

Too late.

The story ends as Gregorio witnesses his father's murder. As a rush of fire and burning energy encompassed him, and at a young age, Gregorio took justice into his own hands. There by a raging river another man lost his life.

What an amazing story, I think in awe. I could see him so clearly in my memory, those eyes, grandpa's eyes, reaping pain and wisdom. Yet what made me love this man so much more was although he was a man's man, he was loving and gentle with his grandchildren.

Every morning became "our" morning; he would strap me into his white Ford Mustang and take me into town to feed his deadly habit. A diabetic, at home he was not allowed anything for his sweet tooth. So upon arriving at his sister's bake shop, he would order me a soft drink, himself something sweet, and pass the time chatting of old times with his sister.

Soon things became bitter. My grandfather died. My four-year-old mind and heart only knew that I missed him terribly and thought it unfair that we had such a short time together.

I knew my grandfather had a strong impact on my father as well. Before my father was thirty, he lost both his parents. It was the first time I ever saw a grown man cry. My father was the other remarkably strong, brave, respectable man in my life. I wished I could take all my father's pain away. I often hear how as a parent you don't want to see your children suffer and wish you could suffer instead. This case was different. I wanted to take my father's pain away, and I knew my father would have rather taken his father's place. What a painful sight, to see a man grieve the loss of a loved one. I could see then the stories of my father that were beginning to be embedded around his eyes—the lines and wrinkles of time.

Things don't really seem as they are until you look back upon them, older and wiser. Now I sit here a granddaughter, a daughter, and soon to be a mother, impatiently awaiting the arrival of one who dwells within me and patiently awaiting the arrival of the lines and wrinkles that will eventually tell my stories.

The College Student, Who Became a Soldier, Who Became a Teacher

Deig A. Sandoval

"We need to help students and parents cherish and preserve the ethnic and cultural diversity that nourishes and strengthens this community and this nation."

—César Chávez

Raised in Edinburg, part of the upper Rio Grande Valley, I finally graduated high school. The size of the Rio Grande Valley allowed most residents to know each other but was still large enough for privacy. As many families in our modern era endure divorce, our family was also afflicted with the divorce disease. "*Me mortifica mi hijo que usted no podrá ir a la Universidad que quiere,*" my mother said sobbing. She rarely spoke Spanish, but when she did, it showed that her emotions were running on high. In keeping with the tradition of being the oldest, I assumed the role of the head of the house while my mother got her wits back. After two years at the local university and a job, I finally saved enough money to attend my original school of choice. Mother gave me my *bendición* as I left the house and began my new adventure.

I drove to San Marcos, tucked away in the beautiful Texas Hill Country. I thought, *This is going to be heavenly place to live. Texas State University is a great environment not only for me to develop academically but socially as well.* Texas State, however, is regarded as a "party school." For me, fresh from the Valley, the challenge was trying to balance college algebra with frat parties, marching band, and excursions with the females of our species.

Success is achieved through many lessons learned from mistakes. The lesson I learned, in relation to physics and hydrology, was the limit of beer cans that can be held in a poorly engineered inner tube while floating down the Guadalupe River. Perhaps if my fellow classmates had paid attention they would have learned that the weight displacement of the beer affects the buoyancy in the water. Other things I learned revolved around planning, tasking, and responsibility. Efficiency is lost after a drive from San Antonio, to Austin, and back to San Marcos for all-night parties. When I left for school, I was not sure where it would take me, but I did know I was about to make the transition from teenager to adulthood.

Once near the cool waters of the San Marcos River, I dipped my feet into the unusually comfortable water warmed by that day's blazing sun and let the currents sweep over my feet. Many students played and sunbathed in the park as they enjoyed the final days of summer. I laid back, totally calm, planning the next move that would ensure I stayed in such a lovely environment. The partly clouded skies broke, the sun shone on my face, and since I was practically blinded, I looked towards the west. When I opened my eyes, there was a break in the thick foliage covering the west gate that led to the football team's practice field. A banner in bold letters read, "TUITION PAID, GO TO COLLEGE FOR FREE!" I leapt to my feet, put my shoes back on, and like the early settlers, headed west into the unknown.

Now, unlike Robert Frost's poem "The Road Not Taken," I mustered up my courage and walked the road and up the steps to room #2 at the Military Entrance Processing Station. Sworn to "...defend and protect the United States and its Constitution against all enemies both foreign and domestic...," at the end of the ceremony, the mounds of signatures, the pricks and probes, the lines, the doctors, rude hosts, getting undressed, dressed, undressed again, the endless "I need your specimen; please fill to this line," I was finally a soldier in the United States Army and a member of the Texas National Guard.

Being a member in the Guard I thought to myself, *I go to school for free and serve my country—WOW! What a deal!* Saturday, August 4 was my first FTX (field training exercise) at Ft. Hood; I got my uniform and whatever gear I needed ready. Joining an artillery unit, I learned how to translate various complicated geometric equations into firing solutions for the artillery cannon. With that experience and exercise, I begin to think, I'll attend school and continue to live off campus. All goes well, the world keeps turning, I am happy in my own little world. I even scheme, reflect to myself, *I wonder if I can get more of those MREs (meals ready to eat): I have run out of food at my apartment. Again!*

I awaken groggy and dazed as my cellular phone rings out the "Mexican Hat Dance." It's Krisy, an old friend from high school, "Oh my goodness! Are you Okay?"

As I wipe the nocturnal drool off my cheek, I mutter, "What are you talking about? Of course I am."

"Planes hit the World Trade Center and the Pentagon!" As she says this I look at the bottom of my TV screen and notice the time and date—September 11, 10:47 am EDT. That day blew the winds of change into my sails and set me on a new path, taking me to distant lands, dangers, and adventures.

Ten days after I left my quiet apartment in San Marcos, I got off a C-130 transport plane surrounded by Air Force security with weapons drawn. We proceeded to load up on buses with bullet proof windows that looked like glass soda bottle bottoms, and we were whisked away through the war-torn country to Camp Bondsteel. "It's showtime!"

The bus ride to camp was humbling, for the people of Kosovo don't have many personal possessions. Their dwellings are partially built, there is trash everywhere, and the scars of war are still present. As we unloaded from the bus to process, "The camp is huge!" I exclaimed. Camp Bondsteel is self-sustained with its own generators, water processing plant, fuel bladders, hospital, and mini airport. The camp buzzed with activity and was not as bad as many of my comrades had thought a designated combat zone would be. Bondsteel has a mini mall, pizza joint, theater, and a world class recreation center with almost anything anyone can think of doing. One thing was for sure, once we were done with our missions for the day, we had something to do back at camp.

The air, warm and thick with moisture, reminded me of the Rio Grande Valley when it rains and doesn't cool off. The Staff Sergeant next to me said, "Specialist, you better be drinking water. I sure wouldn't want to stick ya." I nodded and drank from my hydration system since I did not want to "tabbed out," by a gorilla of a man jousting my vein with an I.V. line to keep me from dehydrating.

First thing that came to mind, *Combat training at Ft. Benning, Georgia sucked!* Second thought went something like this, *Whether it sucked or not, the training would save my life if I got into a predicament in Kosovo.* Surely, I did not want to pass out and miss counter landmine training. Though the war in Kosovo had been silent for several years, the beautiful country side was still peppered with land mines.

"Ruck up!" barked the gorilla super soldier. "Our next lane is weapons training!" After taking a healthy swig from the hydration system, I stood up and felt the blood rush to my new blisters, and my feet began to swell again. These poor plantars endured this feeling once before, during a twenty-five kilometer march in basic training. Lifting my "ruck" (an oversized backpack with many pockets to accommodate clothes, ammunition, food, wet weather gear, a sleeping system, and the occasional kitchen sink—seventy to ninety pounds worth of combat gear), the weight fell into the creases on my back and off we went down a lushly vegetated trail for more training.

KABOOOOOMMMMM! The blast created a shockwave that practically rocked the building off its foundation. Eddie said without a flinch or skip in thought, "Yes...it's quite normal and sometimes they like to use bigger explosives. E.O.D (Explosive Ordinance Disposal) usually blows up all the stuff they find such as mines and weapons. They get to practice their demolition skills." Edmond Halili, a young man who worked for the camp, was born and raised in Kosovo. He was the administrative person and a whiz in the office. Eddie, a fine linguist, spoke Albanian, Serbian, Arabic, French, and the occasional Spanish which he had picked up from the *novellas* of Spain. Having Eddie around our section helped when we escorted VIPs. His knowledge about the area we traveled really helped, especially with four star generals in our care. On one trip, our skills and ability to protect would be put to the test.

We visited a police academy near Pristina. "My goodness, Corporal, it is unusually warm this afternoon," said the Colonel.

There was a bright flash, a wave of heat, with a thunderous crash and boom. Time seemed to stand still then fast forward as the waves of heat and shock struck my body. Random pictures appeared in my mind, then blurred before I could comprehend them. A split second later I heard car alarms and shattering glass everywhere. "Get in the vehicles!" I barked. As I leapt into the vehicle, checking everyone was there, I flipped the ignition, simultaneously counting the other vehicles. *Everyone is good to go*, I thought to myself. The SUVs jerked into gear and we were off like secret spy agents trying to evade capture. My adrenaline began to pump as we maneuvered through the tight European roads, occasionally missing a collision by a chihuahua's hair. Our radio communication was jammed tight with communications going back and forth in a chaotic symphony.

Not all missions were as dangerous or surprising. Our humanitarian mission at a local school was probably where I had my revelation to become a teacher.

Nearing the camp, the commander noticed my hand shaking. "Corporal, I assume when you become a teacher your nerves won't show. I've been told children feed on it in the class like sharks in blood-filled waters," he said flatly.

"No, sir,...I won't shake like this in the classroom; then again I don't believe the students have the capabilities to build bombs," I said nervously with a slight laugh. There was an eerie silence in the vehicle before a soldier began to laugh and then we all did. The stress released into roaring laughter. We felt safe.

Finding out that the teachers there only received 100 Euros a month, which translates to 200 dollars, it was hard to believe they would work for that little. The facilities were not the best, basically walls and a roof. The restrooms had toilets but the waste had nowhere to go but up and out, literally everywhere. There were no bulletin boards and no work by happy productive students. There was merely a posted sign of the rules in Albanian and Serbian. I asked, "Why put up with this job in this condition?"

The aged former soldier and veteran teacher said, "The children are the future of our world. In order to save us from this hellish place and rebuild, we must remove the hate, ignorance, and fear that is festered by the uneducated. With education I fight back. And that is a fight worth fighting. It is all I can do."

I have adopted his words and his flame for teaching. Thanking their dean, teachers, and students, we dropped off their monthly supplies donated by schools in the U.S. On the tranquil drive back to camp I began to think, *If they manage to teach in such conditions, I can go back home. Home sweet home."*

As the plane settles down like an elephant with gentle wings, I'm home. The weight on my shoulders lifts as I grab my carry-on items and deplane. Literally dashing, dodging, and weaving through the ocean of people, I arrive. The elevator is before me. Pausing for a split second, I say to myself, *Hmmm the opposite elevator to back home. Interesting.* Opposite, indeed. I have ended one journey and initiated another.

Trading pistols, bullets, and rifles for pencils, pens, and rulers was a comforting thought. Trading grenades and bayonets for apples and smiles warmed my thoughts and brought a grin to my face as I was greeted by my loving wife, Ana. "How was your flight?" she asked.

"Good, dear. You know something? I think I'm going to become a teacher," I said with a shy smile.

She stopped and said laughingly, "Are you crazy!"

I looked back at her like the farmer in the Asian Zen folklore tale, and answered "Maybe."

Now I have passed all the tests needed to hold the "golden ticket" of certification to teach in Texas. I will be teaching third grade bilingual students in my hometown of Edinburg. My goal is to help them draw out their full potential as leaders and citizens of tomorrow. I hope that under my guidance and because of my experiences, I will be able to spark the inner learning that lives in all children. That fire of knowledge will launch them to positive and fruitful success. I believe every child has the capability to succeed as long as they know they can. I've always believed in the saying, *"El querer es poder."* "Where there is a will, there is a way."

Blue Ride
Through Life
Sandra Silva

His rugged, calloused hands felt soft and warm as he gently wiped the tears from my cheeks. His enormous chest felt like a giant haven protecting me from every danger.

"*Estás bien, mija. Ya no llore, mi niña,*" he softly whispered as he comforted me gently. This macho-like man worried about his baby and would do anything to keep her happy.

"*¡Papá, es que no puedo! Nunca voy la aprender a usar la bicicleta,*" I said sniffling. I sat there on the hot caliche rocks, stubborn with arms crossed.

I didn't understand why my dad wanted me to ride the bicycle without training wheels. I was doing perfectly fine with them—they didn't bother me. As a matter of fact, they even made me go faster, or so I thought. Daddy kissed my wounded, scabbed knee and motioned me to try again.

"*Se me van a salir las tripas, Papi¡ Me voy a desangrar,*" I exclaimed as a protest to getting back on that mechanical bull. This excuse, based on a Mexican myth, was commonly told to children to avoid accidents. Believe me, after the bloodcurdling stories told to us by our parents and older siblings, no child wanted to live their lives without their guts.

My father chuckled, "*Ándale mija, yo sé que tú puedes.*"

"*Pero Papi, no me vaya a soltar. No puedo sin usted a mi lado,*" I agreed conditionally. I felt if Daddy wasn't there to hold me, the mechanical bull would take advantage of his absence and hurt me again.

I raised my aching body off of the hot caliche road and walked toward the opponent. I climbed on. Daddy stayed by my side as he had promised. We practiced several times; Daddy always kept holding on. A couple of days later, we went out to conquer our goal again.

"*¡Ay vas, ay vas! ¡Vas muy bien, no tengas miedo, mija! Yo se que tu puedes,*" Daddy confidently assured me of my progress as I pedaled for my life.

All of a sudden, I couldn't hear my dad panting behind me. That made me worry. *Had Dad fainted from heat exhaustion,* I wondered. *Did he disappear into the caliche road? Where had he gone?*

"*¿Papi? ¿Papi?*" I checked for him frantically.

"*¡Vas muy bien, mija! Vas sola! Qué te dije, tú puedes vencer todas tus metas,*" my dad called proudly from what seemed like miles behind me. I could hardly see him through the caliche dust my furious bike riding had caused.

Wow, I did it! I had accomplished my goal just as Dad had promised. I felt like a free bird soaring through the summer breeze with my long braids floating in midair. This wasn't as hard as I thought. All I needed was confidence, support, and practice.

These words echo in my head and serve as inspiration for my everyday life: "*Vas muy bien, no tengas miedo! Tú puedes vencer todas tus metas.*" "*¡Vas muy bien!*"

As I encounter life's obstacles, these words encourage me and make me feel confident to accomplish anything upon which I set my heart. Even though I came from a humble home, I was taught to be proud of what I was and what I wanted to become. During my high school years, I tried my best, practiced as much as I could, and believed in myself. Despite negative influences, I tried to overcome them and achieved another goal. I graduated in the top ten percent of my class. I made my parents proud, for neither of them had gone beyond an elementary education.

"¡No tengas miedo!"

As I enrolled in college, my dad reassured me that I could handle it and that he'd support my every decision. *"No tengas miedo,"* he said on my first days of school. I wasn't sure if I could do this alone. None of my high school friends went to college. Instead, they'd go out to party and would brag about it when I had to go to the library to research or study. I overcame the fear of being alone and made new friends who shared the same interests as I did. I went through every semester and strived to finish and start my career.

"¡Tú puedes vencer todas tus metas!"

As I stood in line ready to walk down that aisle on May 17, 2003, I reminisced about our bike ride adventure. Wow, I did it. I accomplished my goals, just as Dad had promised. Hey, this was easier than I thought. All the support, confidence, and practice finally paid off.

"Sandra Silva, Bachelors of Interdisciplinary Studies with a specialization in Bilingual Education," the Dean announced. I walked over to him proudly, with my head up high and gave my dad, who was standing in the crowd, a wink.

Autumn in Wisconsin
Hortencia Villa

We had stayed too long up North that year; September had descended, and still we lingered. I cried knowing that once I returned to Donna, I would struggle to catch up with the rest of the students. I always enrolled late in school. As a migrant family, we followed the seasonal crops to earn a living; the welfare of the family unit took precedence over an education.

"Tencha, stop being a baby, and go comb your hair," ordered Mom. "You know that we need the extra money to finish paying off the house and the property taxes."

With my family, financial disaster loomed like thunder clouds threatening hail to ruin the crops. We took advantage of every opportunity that offered work and wages. We labored all summer, praying for good weather, good housing, good wages, and good crops. I tired of the work. I wanted to go home. I wanted to play with my friends. I didn't want to go to school up here. The *viejo*, the gringo *patrón*, told all the families with school age kids to send us to school. "The law will fine me if your kids work in the fields and do not attend school." I had never gone to school up North. The thought of seeing so many Anglo kids in one place scared me. Would they talk to me? Would they like me? Would I like them?

"Tencha, stop being a baby, and make sure you scrub that neck of yours real good."

More than my neck was on the line! My eyes, my skin, my hair, my voice, my tears would be scrutinized. But Mom always says, "Don't let them see you cry; *¡cómete las lágrimas!*" "Them" was the outside world, the sorrows, the fear. To succeed in life we must face our fears and not drown in "them."

The inevitable day arrived. My family sent me to school. The night before, I took out the new school clothes that I had saved for my debut in Donna. The clothes were not meant for Green Bay, Wisconsin in autumn; they were meant for *el valle*, a place for cool bright summer clothes. I did not fit in Wisconsin. I did not speak Wisconsin. I did not eat Wisconsin. I did not believe in Wisconsin. Get me out of Wisconsin!

Mother woke me up early to get ready for school. Happy to wear my new school clothes, I put on my new bright blue tights and penny loafers. *I will look just as stylish as the blond little girls*, I thought. For lunch Mother prepared my favorite *taquitos*, scrambled eggs with sliced wieners and chile sauce. She carefully wrapped them in aluminum foil and put the bundle in one of the Safeway paper bags that she saved for the family lunches. She inspected my grooming endeavors and performed her motherly ritual, one she imparted on her children anytime they left her side.

"*Hortencia, ven para darte la bendición.*" I knelt before her as she solemnly made the sign of the cross. This ritual made me uncomfortable because I got the impression I would die and never see her again.

"*Hortencia, pórtate bien; pon atención a las monjitas.*" She placed her hands on my cheeks and patted them to reassure me that I would do all right. "*A ver, déjame ver esos dientes. ¿Te los lavastes bien?*" I didn't see the benefit of it since I didn't think I would smile or talk that much. "*¿Qué tonterías son esas, Tencha? A ver dáme un besito. Vas a aprender muchas cosas de Dios con las monjitas.*"

But no number of *bendiciones* and *besitos* could rid me of the apprehension I felt in my throat and stomach. Just because I knew a little English by the third grade, my mother thought that I could make my way in an *Americano* world and walk to school alone. My big brother Antonio, who had gone as far as eighth grade, enrolled me in school and drove the home-to-school route a couple times, pointing out points of reference until I had memorized the way from home to school. A long journey awaited me.

"I am sorry, Tenchita, that I cannot drive you to school in the mornings, but I'll come pick you up after school." Antonio spoke these words with mock seriousness and humor, his way of encouraging his baby sister when he thought she could handle the situation. *Why does my family do this to me? They throw me out into the unknown and expect me survive.*

But autumn had come to Wisconsin. What a revelation for me! It was the first time I saw leaves change into a variety of colors. The vivid shades of yellow, browns, reds, and purple created a bouquet of color. They touched me with their mournful beauty. The chill in the air, the smoky smell of decaying leaves, the crunch of leaves underneath my feet filled me with a longing that I did not understand. It made me ache for the warmth and safety of my family; but, at the same time, it exhilarated me to the bone. And so I left my family circle and ventured out among strangers.

As I walked alone along the sidewalk, the thought of my *taquitos* and their warmth kept my mind off the thought of being surrounded by a lot of Anglo kids. They might stare and make comments "*You are too big to be in third grade. Shouldn't you be in the fifth grade?*" And I might defensively reply, "*Yes, but well, and so what?*"

After wandering around the silent halls, I found my way to my assigned classroom. I knocked on the silent door, and a tall, black-robed woman with wings on her head opened it. An eternity stretched between my words and the nun's. She must have seen the fear and uncertainty in my eyes because she took my hand and pulled me into the room. She bent over me and asked my name. With my mouth dry, I managed to whisper my name. I felt the sweat between my shoulder blades, and I turned my right foot debating whether I should run out of the room, down the hall, and never come back. The nun assigned me the third desk from the back in the second to the last row. I didn't know where to focus my line of vision. The students blurred, but I did see individual faces. By mid-morning I wondered whether I could see the world through my sister Esperanza's cool eyes. And I tried to assume what I considered to be her façade. My sister can stare at a person and not blink. Nothing gets to her. But that only worked until I was called on to read. I declared that I had already read the book the students were reading. The nun then called me to her desk to read from another book.

My bravado only lasted until lunch time. The students opened their lunch boxes and took out their neatly wrapped sandwiches and thermoses of milk. I pulled out my greasy paper lunch bag, and under the cover of lunch room chatter, I stole a bite of my taco. Had anyone seen my greasy bag and taco? I did not eat much that day. The next day I deliberately left my lunch at home. The nun (nothing escaped her) noticed that I had no lunch and asked whether I had brought lunch. I quickly replied that I had forgotten it. I had not counted on her solution. She called over one of the students and said, "Amy, give Hortencia your lunch and you can go home and eat." I could not eat someone else's lunch! It was like stealing something that didn't belong to me. What an embarrassment!

"*Amá*, I don't want tacos for lunch; I want baloney on two slices of white bread and add cheese and mayonnaise. That's what all the Anglo kids eat. I don't want them to see your greasy tacos. It's embarrassing." My mother gave me an exasperated look and promised to make some changes. She did make changes. This time she sliced the wieners in half lengthwise, fried them, and put them between the two slices of bread. "*Amá*, not wieners, baloney! These don't look like Americano sandwiches!"

"*Tencha*, you love wieners. *Mira, si tienes hambre te los comes. Con hambre no hay mal taco.*"

Memories of Tía
Myriam Villarreal

As I stood by the doorway I could hear the loud breathing and crying for help. Tears rolled down my eyes so slowly that I felt they created streets on my face. There was nothing I could do but pray. I got on my knees and began sobbing. I asked God, "Why her? She has done nothing to you." My voice trembled with unreasonable questions as I knelt in front of that wooden cross. My body felt hot and full of anger. My mind knew I shouldn't question Him, but my heart needed an answer. I stayed in that small room at the hospital praying for long hours full of anger and questions. When I left the small warm chapel in the hospital, I knew my answer.

She was going to die, and there was nothing else I could do. God had given her to us, and the time for Him to enjoy her in heaven approached. All that would remain with us were memories; those wonderful memories that had been engraved in our hearts forever.

I walked to the lobby area of the hospital, a place that had become my second home. I sat in one of the cold steel chairs that gave me chills, and began remembering.

My mind took me back to Easter Sunday in 1998. The noises of that Sunday after church began to fill my mind: the kids wanting to get in the pool, my cousin Eddie looking for a fork to turn the meat on the grill. His voice filled the house, "I need a fork. *¡Se me va a quemar la carne!*" *Tía* went rushing to help him find a fork so she could stop the storm he was creating over a fork. The rest of us sat in the living room remembering old times, the things we used to do when we were small. *Tía* joined our conversation and we all began talking, laughing, and crying. For a moment it felt like we had never grown up, as if we were still those little kids she loved so much.

I took a deep breath as I stared at the door that led into my aunt's hospital room, and tried to contain my crying, but this time my cry was different. It was a cry of thanks; thanks to God for allowing such moments.

Then I remembered Thanksgiving. That wonderful holiday that filled the kitchen and the entire house with the sweet aroma of hot homemade pecan pie. Thanks to my *Tía*, Thanksgiving had become one of my favorite holidays. On Thanksgiving 1990, she told me the reason we celebrate Thanksgiving. I knew it meant eating turkey and pecan pie, and that was all that mattered to me. But she told me that we celebrate this day because it's an opportunity to give thanks for all the wonderful things we have received all year long. My aunt, a sweet caring person, who always looked after others before herself, always made sure we had a place to spend the holiday. Like magic it seemed we all expected her phone call, the call that would reassure us the invitation was there. As we sat there then, waiting for my parents to get back from the store, she told me, "*te quiero mucho mijita,*" and gave me a warm hug.

December 1998 became the direction of my journey of memories. It had been our last Christmas together as a family with my *Tía*, not only for us but also for her four children and her husband. She organized one of the greatest parties we ever had. Everyone was there—aunts, uncles, cousins, and grandparents. Everything seemed perfect, but I guess we all failed to notice that she was slowly getting sicker. I remember hearing her talking to *Güelita* Mariá about her illness.

"*¡Mija, tienes que ir al doctor!*" commanded my grandma with concern.

"*Estoy bien, tengo anemia, pero ya se me quitará,*" responded my aunt trying to assure my grandmother.

I remember questioning how she had become anemic, but like everyone else, I figured she would eventually get better.

The following Easter, Easter of 1999, was spent at the hospital with an uncertainty of the future. There was no party for the first year since I could remember, and all the happy faces had turned into sad ones. Finally, after a week in hospital my aunt was allowed to go home.

That year my cousin Homer, one of her many nephews, graduated from high school, so we all went to Houston to celebrate with him. The doctors advised my aunt not to go, but she refused to stay. She didn't look good, and we worried about her, but she insisted on going. As we all sat down watching my cousin open his gifts, I took her by the hand and told her "*Tía*, next year is my college graduation, and I want you to make me some delicious pecan pie." She looked at me and said with a soft and sad tone in her voice, "*Ay mijita*, next year I won't be here anymore but know that I love you and that you are very special to me." Then for the last time she gave me long and sweet hug.

I took a deep breath and opened my eyes, as I heard the noise of people walking back and forth. "*Se me murió......que voy hacer.....*" cried my grandmother as she hugged my grandpa wanting him to give her an answer, an answer that he didn't know, for he was suffering as much as she was. *Tío* Abel, my aunt's husband, stood by her side looking at her with more love than ever, his face was full of sadness, yet he seemed to be thanking God for stopping her suffering.

I stood by the doorway one more time, but this time I looked inside and saw my aunt's body, lying there waiting to be taken. Her body was there, but I knew her soul was already in heaven, the place where she belonged. Liver cancer took her at a very young age, forty-five, but it can never take away the memories that will live in my heart forever.

Who I Am
Laura Muñoz Zimmerer

"What do you mean you don't speak Spanish? *¡Eres una Mexicana!* It's who you are," Albert scolded me from the kitchen where he was making rice. He had called to me in Spanish, and I mistakenly volunteered the information that I only understood a few things in my mother tongue, and I couldn't speak it at all.

Explaining that no one in the part of Illinois where I grew up spoke Spanish didn't help the situation. He just kept repeating, "*No me importa. Eres Mexicana*" No excuse worked for him.

Just then, Abel, my boyfriend, walked in. He saw the look on his twin brother's face as he placed the hot-off-the-grill *fajitas* on the counter. "What's wrong?" he asked as he walked over to give me a kiss hello.

"*Tu blah blah blah blah blah español!*" Albert explained with disgust in his voice and on his face as he motioned in my direction. I didn't understand his words, but the tone was enough for me.

"Oh, my poor baby!" Abel smiled as he hugged me close in what seemed like a protective move. "Did I forget to tell you that she is a coconut?" he asked with a sickly sweetness that made my stomach turn.

Albert laughed.

"What's a coconut?" I asked, feeling like I had been insulted just by the sound of his words.

"Someone who is brown on the outside but wants to be white on the inside," Albert bellowed from the kitchen where he had returned to check on his rice.

This time Abel laughed.

"I am not white on the inside," I retorted feeling the sting of his words. "I am Mexican through and through!" I defended myself, proud of my heritage, wanting them to know how I felt.

Abel and Albert gave each other a knowing look. Both from San Benito, I guess they had heard that before. Then Abel squeezed me, letting out a little chuckle before he walked out again to get the rest of the *fajitas*. Albert turned up the radio to hear a block of music by the recently deceased Selena and I think to rub in the fact that he thought of me as a coconut.

I sat on the couch to wait for the rest of my friends to get there. You see, Albert and Abel had the privilege of hosting the BBQ that week. Something that obviously felt old hat to them took the place of the strangest custom I had ever come across.

We would all gather at someone's apartment on a Sunday night. I knew it would have been houses if we weren't all in college in Austin, away from the comforts of home in the Rio Grande Valley. The host took charge of rice and meat and the others all brought some sort of side dish. The girls, except me, would eventually take over the kitchen and the guys would all end up drinking by the BBQ pit. Always the rebel girl, I would go hang out with the guys. Back then I didn't know they saw it as disrespect.

Anyway, as I sat on the couch waiting for the tradition to begin, I thought hard about the term "coconut."

It wasn't that I wanted to be a coconut. I didn't try pushing the Mexican part of me away, but I guess, in a sense you could consider me a coconut. I didn't feel white, though; I felt Mexican. How did this happen? How did I become this...this...dreaded thing called "a coconut?"

Getting lost in my thoughts, I came to the realization that none of this had anything to do with me. I had heard the story hundreds of times, so many times that I could actually picture it in my head. Only then did I realize that my "coconutiness" was caused by events that happened before I was born.

In 1969, in a small suburb of Chicago, a nameless tall Anglo teacher handed my older brother, Bobby, who was four at the time, over to my mother like he had some sort of disease that she thought contagious. Her clear blue eyes could not hide the disdain she felt at the poor job Mom had done raising Bobby.

"Your son cannot come to our school next year. He is retarded," the teacher bluntly announced loudly enough for the crowded room of mothers and children to hear. The mothers, in response, pulled their children closer to them to protect them against the dread of retardation.

"No, he *es* not," my mother replied with indignation in her voice and in the tall, straight-backed, head-up stance she took. She hadn't learned much English as a Mexican child, who only spoke Spanish growing up in the Valley. She knew her English sounded broken and her accent was impossible to hide, but no one, not even this sharply dressed, well-educated women who obviously thought she was better than God, could insult her offspring.

"He is," the teacher adamantly stated reflecting Mom's posture.

"No!" came Mom's one word defiance.

"Yes, he is ma'am," the teacher repeated, this time taking my mother by the shoulders to usher her out of the room.

"Show me," my mother said, standing her ground.

"Well," the teacher began with a roll of her eyes and an exasperated sigh, "for one thing, the most important thing, he couldn't answer any of the questions."

"What questions?" Mom asked, thankful that the teacher spoke enough for the both of them and that her own lack of English did not show.

The teacher's voice grew louder as she rattled off a series of questions that Bobby apparently could not answer. My mother's eyes grew wide as she began to doubt her comprehension of

English. She knew that Bobby could answer all of the questions. She knew because she herself had quizzed him on them.

So she stood a little taller and said loud enough for the other mothers to hear, not caring anymore about how she spoke, only caring about saving her son, "Yes, he can. He *es* esmart. He knows all *de* answers!"

"Calm down, ma'am," the teacher mockingly soothed with a smirk on her face. Why don't *you* show *me?*

And so Mom knelt down in front of Bobby and began:

"*Mijo, ¿Cómo te llamas?*"

"Bobby," my brother replied as his face lit up to the sound of familiar words.

"*¿Cúantos dedos ves?*" Mom asked holding up four fingers.

"*Cuatro,*" Bobby happily replied.

"*Dime los meses,*" Mom commanded.

My brother confidently recited the months of the year to my mother, in Spanish. Mom stood up and aimed a glare that could have killed at the teacher.

The teacher, in reply, smirked and whispered, as if what she had to say was insulting, and it was, but not in the way she thought, "Oh, he only speaks Mexican."

"No," my mother smugly corrected, "he speaks Spanish. He knows. He comes." That last remark, a demand, rather than a question. My mother knew her rights and the rights of her child. He would not get passed over.

Suffice it to say, Bobby went to school that year and did extremely well. Nonetheless, my parents agreed to stop speaking Spanish to their children. None of their offspring would go through that again.

As the memory of the story came to an end, Alma, Norma, and Erica walked in carrying dishes. I could smell the familiar smells of home, garlic, *comino*, cilantro...I missed home, but this really helped. Of course, the girls didn't cook as well as my mom, but I couldn't get any closer.

Wait! If these smells reminded me of home, I must be

Mexican! I had more brown in me than these twin brothers believed.

Excitedly, I began to search my brain, my heart, and my soul for anything to connect me to my heritage. I remembered the times my mom would listen to her "strange" music. Recalling the way she danced around made me smile. I felt closer to my heritage already.

"*¿Qué haces?* What's up, *Chica?*" Alma called out to me as she dropped her dish off in the kitchen.

"Nothing," I said, uncertain whether or not to fill her in on my thoughts. She came from The Valley and spoke Spanish, too. Not wanting to make myself vulnerable to her as well, I refrained.

"Hurry up, let's eat!" Norma said to anyone who listened. "I have to go get dressed. I want to be there by 7:00. I want to get a table...I want to watch the guys walk in!"

"Where are you off to tonight?" I asked. "Another hot date?"

"No, *mija*," Norma had the habit of calling everyone *mijo* or *mija*. "We are going to see *Jaime y los Chamacos*. We told Abel, but he said you two *iban a las* movies. How come you never go dancing with us? Do you not like to dance?

My brain quickly flashed to dances from my childhood. I recalled hoards of people dancing in a giant circle, with their arms moving up and down like an imitation of a chicken.

Then I recalled the events of three weeks ago.

Leonard and Marissa, from work, had been hounding me for weeks to go Tejano dancing with them. Finally Leonard said, "After this, we will never ask you again. You either go with us tonight, or we'll just stop asking you to do anything with us!"

So, I went.

To my amazement no one looked like a chicken. Actually, these people twisted and turned and flipped and, oh, I fell in love with it all. The music of this band called *La Tropa F* made my toes tap, and I yearned to dance like that. Several cute Mexican guys asked me, but I refused to humiliate myself. No way could I do what they could do.

Leonard and Marissa, excited to see my excitement at the end of the night, could not contain themselves. "We know you liked it!" blurted Marissa on the way to the car. Kind of loud, partly because the residual music overcompensation and partly due to the alcohol, she asked, "Do you want to come see Selena with us next weekend?"

I didn't care about her raucousness or her obvious belligerency. I paid no attention to the cute boys staring at us. I only cared about seeing the dance, so I agreed.

Selena's fan club president shot Selena that week, thus the obvious cancellation of the concert. Leonard and Marissa were so inconsolable that I thought I would never get another chance. They seemed to have lost something special by the way they reacted to the news.

It didn't really matter to me that I missed Selena's concert, it would be a long time before I wished that I had gotten the chance to see her. Besides, I had to clean my apartment for a party that I was going to have on Saturday. It was supposed to be a big one, and Marissa had promised to invite a bunch of cute guys that knew how to dance. I didn't understand why she said at the time, because at all of the parties that I had ever been to or had, no one ever danced.

"Hey, what are you thinking about?" interrupted Abel as the thought of that wonderful dancing lingered in my head.

"How come you didn't ask me to go to that dance tonight?" I asked in an accusing tone.

"I know you don't know how and I didn't want to embarrass you," he calmly replied.

Marissa hadn't lied when she said that she was going to tell a bunch of cute guys about my party. Let me tell you, a bunch of cute guys showed up.

Actually, Abel and Albert arrived first. I hadn't met them before that. And yes, they were cute, too.

As the party went on, the atmosphere began to change. The regular people who mulled around and talked to everyone began to leave. Soon only my new friends and the cute guys remained. They quickly pushed all of my furniture against the walls, stacked the chairs, and began to dance. They all danced like the people from the concert I went to with Leonard and Marissa. As a matter of fact, I even recognized some of them.

I guess Abel saw me standing there against a wall with desire in my eyes. He saw the yearning to dance, and he recognized it like a pro.

"Come dance with me," he commanded rather then requested.

"I can't," I sadly stated.

"Is it because you have a boyfriend?" Abel not so subtly asked.

"No," I said, "I really don't know how, I am sorry."

Abel stood by me for the rest of the night. He brought me drinks and made small talk. His attentiveness endeared him to me. So when he left with a request for my phone number, I gladly gave it.

We spent time together everyday. We watched movies, went out to eat, hung out with other friends at their traditional BBQ's, and we even went to a party much like the one I had thrown. Always considerate of my feelings, he would not leave me alone with people he knew would speak to me in Spanish. He became my translator and one of my best friends.

I guess his consideration made him do what he did the night my friends went to see *Jaime y Los Chamacos*. The minute Albert left, Abel began to move the furniture in his small apartment against the walls.

"What are you doing?" I asked.

"You'll see," he replied with a twinkle in his eyes as he brought out his "boom box."

He pressed play and the *Tejano* music blared. Then he held his hand out to me and said, "Will you dance with me?"

I looked at him—hurt. I couldn't believe that this sweet guy, who I had actually started to like, could tease me this way. I shook my head and reached for my purse.

He grabbed me by the hand and said, "I'm serious. I know you want to learn but you don't know how to ask for help. Please let me help you."

And I did.

Abel practiced dancing with me for a few weeks. Then, as he realized I couldn't pick it up from him, he asked Albert to help. The three of us spent every spare minute dancing in a living room from April to December. But I just couldn't get it. I went too fast or too slow. I always missed the beat and my feet would tangle up with theirs; I felt like a failure.

How could I embrace my heritage if the part that called to me most was out of reach? I couldn't.

As my birthday got closer, I could tell that the twins were up to something. They looked at me differently, like they had a secret they could not share.

On the night of my birthday Alma and Norma came over with a pair of Rocky Mountain jeans and a cute shirt. "Happy Birthday!"

"What am I supposed to do with these?" I asked, longing to put them on and magically know how to dance.

Just then, the phone rang. "Did Norma and Alma give you your present yet?" asked the familiar voice on the other end.

"Yes," I said, smiling at the sound of Abel's voice.

"Put it on; I am taking you out!" he commanded.

"Where?" I wanted to know.

"You'll see," he said. I could hear the smile on his lips.

I dressed, boots and all, and Abel came to pick me up. We ended up at a place called *Tejano* Ranch—a dance hall.

Abel held my hand as we walked in, trying to shield my insecurities.

Then I saw all of my new friends sitting at a table with a sign that read: RESERVED FOR LAURA MUÑOZ AND GUESTS.

After a few drinks, my courage grew. Abel must have seen it because he asked me to dance. He held my hand all the way to the dance floor, the way his traditional mother had taught him. Letting me listen to the beat for awhile, he waited before he began to dance.

I don't know if I should give credit to the drinks or to my learning process finally kicking in, but I did it. I really did it and I did it well (if I must say so myself)!

That night my new friends claimed me as one of their own. No longer the coconut, I began my journey to becoming a full fledged Mexican.

I embraced my heritage by learning to cook traditional Mexican meals, making an effort to learn Spanish, and continuing to dance. Now I cannot imagine living any other way.

It has become who I am.

Glossary
OF WORDS, PHRASES, AND CLAUSES

Spanish • English translation/equivalent

A fuerzas ni los zapatos entran. • Not even shoes will go on by force.

A lo mejor hallas piojos. • Maybe you'll find lice.

A ver, déjame ver esos dientes. ¿Te los lavaste bien? • Let's see, let me see your teeth. Did you brush them well?

Abuela/Abuelo • Grandmother/Grandfather

Acércate y come con nosotros. • Come close and eat with us.

adios good-bye

¡Aguas con el venado! ¡Trucha! • Careful with the deer! Watch out!

Ah, que mi Pedro. • Oh, that Pedro of mine.

¡Ahi viene el bus! • Here comes the bus!

Ahi voy • I'm coming.

Ahi voy, Amá • I'm coming, Ma

Ahora ¡qué quiere ese viejo! • Now what does that man want!

ajo and comino • garlic and cumin

algodón • cotton

amá • mom

Amá, ¡aquí tiene sus gallinas! • Ma, here are your chickens!

ancianita • old lady

ándale apúrale • come on, hurry up.

¡Ándale güercos! • Move it, kids!

Ándale, mija, ¡yo sé que tú puedes! • Come on, mija, I know you can do it!

Ándale • Go on, hurry

Anduve buscando hasta que encontré de dónde venía el olor. • I looked until I found where the smell was coming from.

Aquí está vamos a ver. • Here it is, let's see.

Aquí, mijo • Here, son.

arroz con pollo • rice and chicken

¡Ay buey! • literally, ox...figuratively, an epithet used in anger to mean anything from dummy to idiot, or playfully to mean dude, dog, homeboy/girl

Ay ¿cuánto se puede gastar? • Oh, how much can we spend?

¡Ay vas, ay vas! Vas muy bien, no tengas miedo, mija. Yo sé que tú puedes. • There you go, there you go! You're doing very well, don't be afraid, baby. I know you can do it.

Ay, ¡Dios mío! Mija, ¿qué te pasó? ¿Estas bien? • Oh my God! Dear, what happened to you? Are you all right?

Ay, Dios mío, ¡ayúdame! • Oh, my God, help me!

Bájate de allí muchacha, te vas a caer. • Get down from there, girl, you're going to fall.

barrio • neighborhood

bella Rosita • beautiful little rose

bendición • blessing
Bien, bien, vamos a ver. Aquí tengo todos los papeles. • OK, OK, let's see. I have all the documents here.

bodega • packing shed, packing house, warehouse

buenas noches • good evening or good night

Bueno y ¿qué prisa traes? • Well, and why are you in such a hurry?

Bueno, Mamita • OK, Mama

Bueno, ya me voy a bañar. • All right. I am going to take a bath now.

cabrones • literally, male goats...figuratively, any level of a variety of epithets ranging from pest at its mildest to bastard at the strongest. On page twenty-eight, it is used playfully.

Cada lunes, como un reloj suena a tiempo, mis dos hermanas me traían las cartas de Pedro, después de su viaje al mercado. • Every Monday, like clockwork, my two sisters would bring me Pedro's letters, after their trip to the market.

Cada que miro mis jacales me acuerdo de mis gallinas. • Whenever I see my sheds I think of my chickens.

caliche • lime pebbles
calzones • panties

Cámbiate y lávate las manos para que comas. • Change [clothes] and wash your hands so you can come eat.

camisa • shirt

cantinera • barmaid

cantos • songs

Caras vemos, corazones no sabemos. • We see their faces, but know not their hearts. Equivalent to: You can't tell a book by its cover.

cebollas • onions

cervezitas • beers

chachalaca • a bird native to the Valley; their birdcall sounds like the name they have been given; if you call a person a chachalaca, you call him/her a chatter-box.

chicharra • cicada

chicharrones • fried pork rinds

¡Chingones! • He-men!

Chiquita • little one

cholo • gangster

cohetes • firecrackers

colonia • rural, unincorporated, often unregulated area that has been haphazardly developed, often with few if any utilities *comadre /compadre* • literally, co-mother/co-father, it contains a relationship between adults when one is the sponsor for the baptism (or other sacrament) of the child of another. The sponsor becomes madrina or padrino to the child, but comadre or compadre to the parent(s) of the child.

comadritas • pals, friends

comal • griddle

cómete las lágrimas • literally, swallow your tears; figuratively, don't let them see you cry.

comino • cumin

¿Cómo puedes ver tan lejos? • How can you see so far?

con Diosito • with God

con mucho orgullo • very proudly

corrido • ballad

costales • sacks

Cuando el río suena, es que piedras lleva. • When you can hear the river, it is carrying along some rocks. Equivalent to: Where there's smoke there's fire.

¿Cuántos dedos ves? • How many fingers do you see?

cuánto eses • how-much-is-it

cuatitas • twin daughters (fraternal twins)

Cuatro • Four

cuentos • stories

cuernitos • horn-shaped sweet bread

curandera • healer

curándola de susto • curing her for shock

Del dicho al hecho • Between saying and doing...

Del plato a la boca se cae la sopa. • Between the plate and one's mouth, the soup is spilled.

dicho • saying, adage, aphorism

Dime los meses • Name the months for me.

Dios ¡mándame un dotor! • God send me a doctor!

Dios sólo nos da lo que podemos manejar. • God gives us only what we can handle.

Doña • term of respect for a woman

¡Dotor! ¡Dotor! ¿Dónde está el dotor? Que no me toque nadie, ¡nomás el dotor! • Doctor! Doctor! Where is the doctor? Nobody can touch me except the doctor!

el otro lado • the other side of the Rio Grande River—Mexico

El Patrón • the boss

el Presidente • President

El que a buen árbol se arrima, buena sombralo cobija. • The one who goes near a good tree is covered by good shade.

El que con lobos se junta, a aullar se enseña. • If you mix with wolves, you learn to howl.

El que ríe al último, ríe mejor. • He who laughs last, laughs best.

El señor que me deja el periódico es mi amigo. El me trae todos los cupones que le sobran. Vanessa también me trae periódicos de toda la vecindad. Yo no sabía de donde los estaba trayendo, pero Don José me vino a decir que pescó a Vanessa con su periódico. Le tuve que pagar el papel. • The man who delivers my newspaper is my friend. He brings me all the coupons that he has left over. Vanessa also brings me papers from the whole neighborhood. I did not know where she was getting them, but Don Jose came to tell me that he caught Vanessa with his newspaper. I had to pay him for the paper.

en sus tiempos • in her time—in her youth

¡Eres una Mexicana! • You are a Mexican!

Es bueno para él. Lo hará un hombre. • It's good for him. It'll make him a man.

¿Es temprano? Así pensaba yo. Bueno. Yame voy a acostar. Gracias. Me hablas, ¿eh? • It's early? I thought so. OK. I am going to lie down. Thank you. You call me, OK?

¡Ese sí que era un galán • Now that one really was a handsome man!

Espérame para ir contigo. • Wait for me so I can go with you.

Está bien, mijo. • All right, son.

Estas bien, mija. Ya no llore, mi niña. • You're fine, baby. Don't cry any more, my girl.

¡Estas chiflada! ¡Mami te tenía muy chiflada! • You're spoiled! Mom spoiled you!

Estas son las mañanitas que cantaba el rey David. • This is the morning greeting that King David used to sing. See entry for *Las Mañanitas.*

Estas son las mañanitas...ya se metió • first verse of *Las Mañanitas,* a traditional celebration song. See entry for *Las Mañanitas.*

Este anillo fué el que tu abuelo me mandó ese día. • This is the ring your grandfather sent me that day.

Estos viejos mensos. Mira lo que hicieron. • These stupid men. Look what they did.

Estoy bien, tengo anemia, pero ya se me quitará. • I'm fine, I'm anemic, but it will go away.

familia • family

frutos de su trabajo • fruits of his labor

gorditas • thick corn flour griddle cakes that, after cooking, are filled with any prepared food.

Gracias • Thank you

¡Gracias a Dios! ¡Gracias Dotora! • Thank God! Thank you, Doctor!

grito • yell

gritos de alegria • shouts of joy

Güelita • Grandma

güeros • literally, fair-skinned ones; figuratively, as used here, anglos or *gringos*

hasta luego • until later; until then; until we meet again

Hazme caso—tienes que esperar antes que salga el sol. • Listen to me—you have to wait until right before sunrise.

Hermanos mayors • older siblings

hija/hijo • daughter/son

Hola • hello

hombre • man

Hoy iré a pedir tu mano para que nos puédanos casar. • Today, I will go ask for your hand so that we may be married.

iban a las movies • were going to the movies

Juani ¿puede salir Sara a jugar? • Juani, can Sara come out to play?

la bendición • the blessing

la consentida/el consentido • the favorite child, often the youngest, and often spoiled by everyone who is older

La Raspa • traditional Mexican folk dance

la rosita mas bella en Tejas • the prettiest rose in Texas

La vida en el barrio, qué sabrosa. • Life in the barrio, how delectable.

La Virgen María • the Virgin Mary

las gallinas • the chickens

Las Mañanitas • literally, the early mornings…traditionally, a song for birthdays, saints days, mother's days, any special day

las noticias • the news

lavamanos • lavatory

le besan la mano • kiss her hand

leno • log, piece of wood or branch

levántate • get up

limón, tamarindo, papaya, or fresa • lime, tamarind, papaya, or strawberry

Lo que menos puedes ver, en tu casa lo hasde tener. • That which you can't stand, you'll wind up having to live with.

Los muchachos no podían venir a sacarnos • Boys couldn't come to take us out on a date.

Los Reyes Magos le dieron una cobija al Santo Niño Dios para que no tenga frío durante el año. • The Magi gave the holy baby God a blanket so that He will not be cold during the year.

Ma ¿dónde chingaos está mi pellet gun? • Mom where the hell is my pellet gun?

machismo • manly

Magdita, te voy a estar viendo desde la ventana de la cocina, nadamás no le vayas a dar muy recio porque te puedes caer y lastimar. ¿Está bien? • Magdita, I am going to be watching you through the kitchen window; just don't swing too fast because you can fall and hurt yourself. All right?

Mamá, ¿qué hizo? • Mama, what did you do?

mamá's plancha • mother's iron

Mami, ¿dónde estas? • Mommy, where are you?

mañana • morning; tomorrow

Me dijeron que sí, como quiera las tiran. • They told me that they throw them away anyway.

buscar un anciano para cuidar y ganar mucho dinero como mi comadre Amparo. • look for an old person to take care of, and earn lots of money like my *comadre Amparo*

Me mortifica mi hijo que usted no podrá ir a la Universidad que quiere. • I am worried, my son, that you will not be able to go to the University you want to attend.

mercado • market

Mi desierto • My desert

Mi hijita • my little daughter

Mi viejita • my old lady

Mija, he estado pensando. ¿Por qué no vamos a las garage sales en Houston un fin de semana? • Dear, I've been thinking. Why don't we take a week-end trip to the garage sales in Houston?

Mija, mira allá está una garage sale! • Daughter, look there is a garage sale!

Mija, nomás me falta un número para ganar el Bingo Wingo • Daughter, I only need one number to win the Bingo Wingo

Mija, ¡tienes que ir al doctor! • Daughter, you have to go to the doctor!

Mijita, (mijito) • literally, my little daughter/son. When used by non-relatives, it's like saying dear or my dear.

Mijo, ¿Cómo te llamas? • Son, what is your name?

Mira, si tienes hambre te los comes. Con hambre no hay mal taco. • Look, if you're hungry you will eat them. If you're hungry, there is no bad taco.

Mojados estúpidos • stupid wetbacks

molcajete • Mexican mortar and pestle, made of lava rock

Mole y arroz con pollo • mole and rice with chicken

mollete, a.k.a. concha • a round Mexican sweet bread, light and airy, with a crumb topping that is shaped in swirls or like a shell

monte • woodland (in the Lower Rio Grande Valley of Texas, the woodlands are populated by mesquite trees and shrubs, Texas Ebonies, *huisache*, cacti, Sabal palms, along with various beneficial and noxious herbs and grasses, often with spiny branches–not to mention the insects, reptiles, birds, and mammals.

muchacho • boy

muchas gracias • thank you very much

¡Muévete, quítate! • Move! Get out of the way!

muy chistoso • very funny

Nadie • Nobody

¿Necesitas algo, Suegro? • Do you need something, Father-in-law?

N'hombre. Puro pedo. • No way. That's BS.

Ni te puedes limpiar la cola y ya anda ahi de fantasioso...Quiero ser doctor. Muy chingón. • You can't even clean your behind and you're creating fantasies...I want to be a doctor. Big shot.

No creo. • I don't think so.

¿No hay gente? ¿Me levanto ya? • Is anybody there? Do I get up now?

No hay necesidad. • It's not necessary.

No me caigo. • I won't fall.

No me importa. Eres Mexicana. • I don't care. You're Mexican.

No puede, tiene que estudiar la Biblia...nos vamos a ir dentro de un ratito... tiene que limpiar la casa... tiene que ayudar a preparar la cena. • She can't, she has to study the Bible ...we are leaving in a little bit ... she has to clean the house... she has to help prepare supper.

No puedo • I can't

No sé, hijo. • I don't know son.

No sé. La señora nomás me la dejó. • I don't know. The woman just left her with me.

No sirvo pa'nada. • I am good for nothing.

No, gracias, no tengo dinero. • No thanks, I don't have any money.

No, Mamita, no se ha bañado. • No, Momma, you haven't taken a bath.

No, todavía no. • No, not yet.

Nomás voy al trabajo. Ándele, vamos. • I'm just going to work. Come on, let's go.

Nos llevamos a los niños. • We'll take the kids.

Ojos que no ven, corazón que no siente. • What you don't know can't hurt you.

olla de barro • earthenware pot

Órale Chuy apúrale vamos a estar late. • Come on, Chuy, hurry up, we're going to be late.

Padre y Esposo Adorado • Beloved Father and Husband

paletas • frozen treat bars, made of ice cream or frozen fruit

palote • rolling pin

Papá, ¡es que no puedo! Nunca voy a aprender a usar la bicicleta. • Papa, I can't! I'll never learn how to ride a bicycle.

para parir • to give birth

para ti mami • for you, mommy

Parece día de muerto en Santa Rosalía • It's like the day of the dead in Santa Rosalia—nothing moving but the wind

Pedo me quiere pegar • Pedo (Pedro) wants to hit me.

periódico • newspaper

pero • but

Pero cuando lo ví por primera vez, yo sabía que él sería mi esposo. • But the first time I saw him, I knew he would be my husband.

Pero Papi, no me vaya a soltar. No puedo sin usted a mi lado. • But daddy, don't let me go. I can't do it without you by my side.

Pero si ya te quieres meter tú y hacer tus cosas, nos podemos meter. • But if you want to go in to do your own things, we can go on inside.

piñatas • big, candy-filled hanging ornament designed to be broken by the children at a birthday party.

platicar • chat, converse

pomada • ointment or salve

Por eso no tengo nadie que me mande. • That's why I don't have anyone who can tell me what to do.

Por estar al pendiente de la maldita comida descuidé a la niña. No debí dejarla jugar sola. Perdóname dios mío. • I neglected my daughter to prepare that blasted meal. I shouldn't have let her play alone. Forgive me, my God!

por favor • please

Porque se oye cuando corre el agua, Mama. Ándele, báñese antes que se levante Chuy. • Because we can hear when the water is running, Mama. Go on, take your bath before Chuy gets up.

pórtate bien; pon atención a las monjitas. • behave yourself; pay attention to the nuns.

Pos no sé. • Well, I don't know.

pueblito • little town

Pues ¿cómo? ¿Que hiciste? ¿Por qué te bajaste? Ay, este señor me va a matar. • Well, how? What did you do? Why did you get down? Oh, this man is going to kill me.

pulga, as in the pulga or la pulga • flea market

Qué bueno que vinieron todos, hoy. Mañana vienen para celebrar el cumpleaños de Andrea. • It's good that you all came over today. Come tomorrow to celebrate Andrea's birthday.

Que chingados sabes de medicina. • What the hell do you know about medicine.

¿Qué creen? ¿Que el dinero crece en árboles? • What do you think? That money grows on trees?

que la sangre de Cristo te cubra • May the Blood of Christ cover you (protect you)

¿Qué tanto pagaste por estas cosas? Yo los puedo hacer. • How much did you pay for these things? I can make them.

Que te bajes de digo. • I'm telling you to get down from there.

Qué te dije, tú puedes vencer todas tus metas. • What did I tell you, you can conquer all your goals.

¿Qué tonterías son esas, Tencha? A ver dáme un besito. Vas a aprender muchas cosas de Dios con las monjitas. • What foolishness is this, Tencha? Come on, give me a kiss. You are going to learn many things about God from the nuns.

¿Que? • What?

Querida • Beloved

Quieren oir los especiales, hoy tenemos nuestra Milanesa a $7.99. • You want to hear the specials; today we have our Milanesa for $7.99.

¿Quieres almorzar? • Do you want to have breakfast? Note: in Castillian Spanish, *almorzar* refers more to having lunch than breakfast, but in the Valley, it refers to breakfast.

quinceañera • fifteenth-birthday celebration, similar to a sweet-sixteen signifying the girl's entry into adulthood

rebozo • long narrow stole

recetas • prescriptions, or recipes

Recuerda que no eres monedita de oro para caerles bien a todos. • Remember that you are not a gold coin made to please everybody.

ropa usada • used clothes

San Martin de Porres, el Santo Niño de Atocha, la Guadalupana, and la Virgen de San Juan ... el Sagrado Corazón • St. Martin de Porres, the Holy Child of Atocha, Our Lady of Guadalupe, and Our Lady of San Juan...the Sacred Heart of Jesus—all icons popular in Mexican American homes.

sandías • watermelons

Se me murió...qué voy hacer... • She has died...What am I going to do?

¡Se me va a quemar la carne! • The meat's going to burn.

¡Se me van a salir las tripas, Papi! ¡Me voy a desangrar! • My intestines are going to come out, Daddy! I am going to bleed to death!

señor • sir, mister

señora • lady or ma'am

Señora Ramirez, vine por mis gallinas. • Mrs. Ramirez, I came for my chickens.

sí • yes

Sí Mamá. • Yes, Mama.

Si tan solo me hubieras escuchado. • If only you had listened to me.

Si tu supieras como sufro por tus besos. • If you knew how I suffer for your kisses.

Sí, Mamá, yo le hablo. • Yes, Mama, I will call you.

Sí, Mami. ¡Ya voy! • Yes, Mommy. I'm coming!

Sí, mija. Apaga la luz, por favor. • Yes, daughter. Turn off the light, please.

sin ti • without you

solamente tu abuela lo haría • only your grandmother would do such things

Soy Marta. Aquí estoy. • It's Marta. I'm here.

¡Súbete, muchacha! ¿Vas a ir, sí o no? • Get in, girl! Are you going, yes or no?

suegra/suegro • mother-in-law/father-in-law

tamales • savory or sweet steamed cakes made of corn flour and stuffed with anything from meat to cheese to beans. Traditional festive food, especially at Christmas time.

Tas loco. • You're crazy.

té de manzanilla • chamomile tea

Te dí el nombre de San Andrés...Naciste el día 30 de Noviembre que es el día de San Andrés. • I named you for St. Andrew...you were born on November 30, which is the feast day of St. Andrew.

Te dije que te bajaras. Este árbol está muy alto. • I told you to get down. This tree is too tall.

¡Te estoy viendo! • I'm watching you!

te quiero mucho mijita • I love you very much my dear daughter

¿Te vas a ir? ¿Por qué? • You're leaving? Why?

Tenga paciencia. • Be patient.

Tengo sueño, era muy tarde anoche cuando nos metimos. • I'm sleepy, it was very late last night when we went in.

terca/terco • stubborn

¿Tienes hambre, Palomo? • Are you hungry, Palomo?

¿Tienes hambre? • Are you hungry?

¿Tienes sueño? Si nomas te metiste y te dormiste. Ni siquiera te bañaste anoche. Te puedo oler. • You're sleepy? But you just went in and went to sleep. You didn't even take a bath last night. I can smell you.

Tío/Tía • Uncle/Aunt

Todavía no, Mamá • Not yet, Mama.

Todo va a estar bien. Dice el doctor que solo fué un raspón. Pronto se le cicatrizará. Yaverás y al rato va andar jugando de nuevo. • Everything will be all right. The doctor says that it is just a scratch. It will scab over soon. You'll see that in a little while she will be playing again.

torero • bullfighter

tortillas • griddle-baked flat bread made of wheat or corn flour

tortillas de harina • wheat flour tortillas

tortillas recién hechas • freshly made tortillas

tres flores • three flowers

tres mojaditos • three wetbacks

Tu eres mi baby, Mijo. • You are my baby, Son.

¡Tú nomás dale! • You just drive!

Tú nomás héchatela. A ver, tómate esta pastilla. A ver si te jala. • You just take it. Let's see, take this pill. Let's see if it works.

tú todo el tiempo piensas lo peor • you always think the worst

Un día, finalmente llegó esa carta que yo tanto añoraba. • Finally, one day I received the letter I longed for.

un vaso nuevo • a new vessel

Una muchacha debía de ser rogada, no rogona. • A girl should be begged, not be a beggar.

Vale más saber que tener. • It is better to know than to have.

¡Vas sola! • You're on your own!

ven • come

Ven p'acá, perrito. • Come over here, doggy.

Ven para celebrar tu cumpleaños, mija • Come to celebrate your birthday, dear.

ven rapidito • come quickly

Ven, para sacudirte. • Come, let me dust you off.

Venga conmigo, Mamá. • Come with me, Mama.

Vente, Palomo • Come on, Palomo.

vestido • dress

wela/welo • grandma/grandpa

Wela, ¿ya se quiere meter para adentro? • Grandma, do you want to go inside already?

Welita, short for Abuelita • Grandma

wewones • lazybones

Y esta, ¿quién es? • And who is this one?

Y tú, ¿cómo sabes? • And how do YOU know?

Ya es hora, Mamita. Levántese y dése un baño. • It's time, Momma. Get up and take your bath.

Ya está lista, Mamá. Vámonos. • You're ready, Mama. Let's go.

¡Ya estan las gallinas ! • The chickens are done!

Ya me bañé. • I already took a bath.

¿Ya me levanto? ¿Me levanto ya? • Should I get up? Do I get up now?

Ya me voy muy lejos del pueblo, empacando maletas aguardando recuerdos de amor…Ya me voy hacia el norte, dejo novias, mis calles, mi gente, mi México,… ay ay ay… algún día volveré… ay ay ay… te prometo mi amor… no lloraré mientras camino…el desierto y la luna…se vienen conmigo • I am going far from town, packing suitcases, keeping memories of love…I am going to the north, I leave girlfriends, my streets, my people, my Mexico, oh, oh, oh…I'll return one day, oh oh oh…I promise, my love…I will not cry as I travel…the desert and the moon come with me.

Ya no llores, todo estará bien hijita. • Don't cry any more; everything will be fine, baby.

¡Ya viene el doctor! • The doctor is coming.

Yo sé en dónde estan los periódicos de ayer. • I know where yesterday's papers are.

Yo sé, Chiquita. • I know, little one.

Yo siempre juraba que cuando yo tuviera una familia de mí propio, que ellos no tendrían que luchar como hicimos. • I always swore that when I had my own family, that they would not have to struggle like we did.